MEETING OF THE MINDS:
THE SOCIAL ENTREPRENEUR'S ROADMAP
FOR COLLABORATIONS THAT WORK

Danielle CARRUTHERS

Solène PIGNET

ISBN 13 : 978 1530345410

TABLE OF CONTENTS

Preface 4

Introduction 6

Scope of this Book...9

To make the best use of this book: 10

A Word of Caution 10

Chapter 1 - The Landscape of Collaborations & Partnerships 12

When to Collaborate..14

Understanding The Problem 15

The 5 Influences of Collaborative Relationships.....................16

Types of Collaborations...24

CHAPTER 2 - Collaboration Roadmap 34

Step # 1 - Get Clarity 38

Step # 2 - Reach Out..40

Step # 3 - Seal the Deal 45

Step # 4 - Drive It Forward (or Not!) 48

Chapter 3 - Case Study: The Global Social Entrepreneurs Lab..................52

Setting the Stage 54

Getting to Know Each Other 55

Beginning an Informal Collaboration 55

Growing..55

Formalizing a Partnership 56

Reflecting on Key Success Factors 57

Chapter 4 - The 6 Most Common Collaboration Pitfalls 60

   Pitfall #1 - Collaborating "Just Because" 63

   Pitfall #2 - Misalignment of Goals 65

   Pitfall #3 - Miscommunication and Misunderstandings 67

   Pitfall #4 - Lack of Direction or Leadership 69

   Pitfall #5 - Clashing Work Styles 71

   Pitfall # 6 - Lack of Formalization 72

Chapter 5 - Top 10 Collaboration Best Practices 78

   #1 - Work on Your Contribution 81

   #2 - Don't Put All Your Eggs in One Basket 81

   #3 - Stay Clear on Your Goals and Objectives 82

   #4 - Be Transparent 83

   #5 - Communicate Clearly, From the Beginning 84

   #6 - Communicate Clearly, When Things Go Bad 84

   #7 - Communicate Clearly, When Things Go Well 85

   #8 - Be Committed 86

   #9 - Think Win/Win/Win 87

   #10 - Build Collaborations with Genuine, Authentic Motives 88

Chapter 6 - Looking Towards Collaboration on a Larger Scale 90

   Joint Ventures 93

      Grameen Danone Foods Ltd. 94

   Collective Impact 96

      Collective Impact Case Study: First 2000 Days 97

   Further Readings 103

Conclusion 105

BONUS RESSOURCES 110

PREFACE

One of the first things we are taught when studying and reading about business, marketing, or entrepreneurship, is to analyze the market conditions. Are there a lot of potential clients? Are there already a lot of competitors?

In impact-oriented entrepreneurship, those questions need to be reformulated.

> It is not so much about how many potential clients there are, but what problems need to be solved. Who are the beneficiaries that can be positively impacted, and how?

> It is not so much about how many competitors there are in the ecosystem, but how the system can be improved collaboratively to better serve those within it.

Instead of thinking clients and competitors, social entrepreneurs think beneficiaries and cooperation opportunities. At least in theory!

Indeed, we are growing in a world where competition is more prevalent than cooperation. From school on, we are taught to perform individually in order to win the competition of grades, schools, jobs and more.

For social entrepreneurs to embrace cooperation is not as easy as it sounds. Our social norms push us to compare our work with alternatives, fear others who are going in the same direction as us, or fear looking small when getting started (as compared to 'them').

It's as if we need to always perform 'on top' or 'ahead' of others.

This book is the perfect example of how so-called competitors can collaborate. Because you see, before joining forces (and creating an event, then a community, then writing this book together!), we used to each work separately on our own initiatives.

Danielle, the founder of theSedge.org, offers online courses for current and aspiring social entrepreneurs. Solène, the founder of Creators for Good, offers individual accelerator programs for current and aspiring social entrepreneurs. They are two different approaches with one shared goal: to support social entrepreneurs with tools and methodologies to maximize chances of success and potential for great impact!

We could have followed what the other was doing from a distance (and actually, we did that for a while). We could have gotten scared when the other launched something brilliant that had the potential to attract too much of our beneficiaries' attention. We could have crossed our fingers for people to choose our solution over the other.

Instead, we started collaborating. Little by little, our impact grew in ways we could not have imagined. Writing a book is far outside both our comfort zones. But together we found the strength, resources, and boldness to write this book for YOU!

Our hope is this book will be the resource you need to thrive too, to drive your impact forward with collaborations: THE secret weapon of Social Entrepreneurs.

Danielle Carruthers & Solène Pignet

INTRODUCTION

*"We're in this together,
and if we united and we inter-culturally cooperated,
then that might be the key to humanity's survival."*

Jeremy Gilley, TEDTalks lecture

As you most likely know from first-hand experience, collaborating and partnering is easier said than done. It may even fail more often than it works.

But social entrepreneurs, impact innovators, and changemakers all have a responsibility to try. Because when it works, collaboration can result in a greater impact on the world around you than you could possibly imagine! Michael Sampson describes collaboration as "people working with other people towards a common outcome." [1]

From a few individuals working together to deliver a one-time event to large ventures establishing lifelong partnerships to deliver a new product or service, joining forces allows changemakers to tackle increasingly complex system-wide challenges.

Despite some in the social sector sharing a view that the term 'collaboration' itself has been overused to the point of diminishing its meaning, the majority would still agree that at its core collaboration is both necessary and valuable in achieving wide-scale social impact.

The scale and complexity of most social and environmental issues are so large that no one person or organization can possibly do it alone.

---

[1] *"Defining Collaboration – 1. The 3P's of Collaboration", Michael Sampson Blog, February 24, 2011,
https://michaelsampson.net/2011/02/24/defining1/*

Sure, everyone can make a separate dent in the universe to improve a cause they care about. But *really* moving the needle and disrupting an unfair, unjust status quo to create a new, more equitable state of being often requires the magic of collaboration.

Collaboration is perhaps the social entrepreneur's greatest 'secret weapon'. Organizing multiple partners in the pursuit of achieving greater social impact creates value in a few unique ways.

1. It allows you to stick to your strengths.

As the old saying goes, 'jack of all trades, master of none'. With collaboration, you can bring together the 'masters' of all the trades you need to get the job done, without compromising on quality. Collaboration allows you to join forces with others who have different strengths than you in order to fill in the gaps in your work with the contribution of others who excel those areas.

2. It means you can diversify what you offer or how you offer it.

Because each individual or organization brings a unique set of skills to the table, collaboration allows you to deliver value in ways you might not be able to on your own.

Working with individuals from diverse points of view brings the opportunity to see problems through new eyes and to listen to new ways of approaching challenges. Asking new questions with new people can lead you down a path you never imagined existed, and sometimes this is how the best breakthroughs show up.

3. It's an innovative way to operate.

A distinctive factor of entrepreneurship is that you are creating value from scarce resources. The main resources, of course, being time and money.

Collaboration allows you to essentially do more with less. Instead of getting a loan to hire new staff to plan and launch a new arm of your work, you can choose to partner with an existing team that has extra bandwidth to plan and launch the same project with you.

4. It's a dynamic way to grow your team.

You can grow the productive hours of your team without hiring employees or contractors. Choosing to partner with other individuals or organizations that have aligned goals means that tasks needing more human resources power can be completed without formally growing your team.

5. It helps you grow your impact.

The most important reason of all. Collaborating helps you grow the breadth and/or depth of your impact thanks to all of the reasons above.

"In spite of current ads and slogans, the world doesn't change one person at a time. It changes as networks of relationships form among people who discover they share a common cause and vision of what's possible."

Margaret Wheatley and Deborah Freize

SCOPE OF THIS BOOK

This is not an academic book on collaboration. It is a practical roadmap to help individual social innovators and small social purpose organizations navigate collaboration and partnership opportunities.

The most important goal when sitting down to write this book was to share ideas that would increase the effectiveness of your efforts to grow your impact through this beautiful, dynamic, and sometimes elusive, 'secret' superpower of collaboration and partnerships.

To make the best use of this book:

- Consider the main impact outcomes you are trying to achieve and keep them top of mind.
- Take lots of notes as you go, stopping to reflect on the questions posed throughout the book.
- If you find yourself puzzling over something that is not addressed, post your question in the Global Social Entrepreneurs Lab and get more insight from your peers in social change.

A Word of Caution

Collaboration is messy. It's messy because we are all human and relationships can get messy! This book was designed as a practical guide because, although the spirit of collaboration is such an important value to social entrepreneurs, it can be really (really) tough sometimes.

Try not to over-analyze the process, and trust us when we say, "don't worry about doing it *all* right *all* at once!".

It's going to take some trial and error, and missteps will most certainly be made along the way. But, that is part of the process. And unfortunately (as much as we wish this weren't true) even the BEST book will never be able to fully eliminate the risk of failing.

You don't need to read this all in one sitting, or to follow the advice perfectly. Use it as a rough guide and framework.

Trust that you already have all the answers you need to build the amazing collaborative relationships that will allow you to scale your impact by leaps and bounds.

"The lightning spark of thought generated in the solitary mind awakens its likeness in another mind."

Thomas Carlyle

CHAPTER 1

The Landscape of Collaborations & Partnerships

CHAPTER 1 - THE LANDSCAPE OF COLLABORATIONS & PARTNERSHIPS

"There are two questions that we have to ask ourselves. The first is 'Where am I going?' and the second is 'Who will go with me?'"

Howard Thurman

As a species who craves connection and community, collaboration comes naturally to human beings. But what exactly does it mean to collaborate? And what does it really look like? How can we collaborate with enough purpose and planning to mitigate the risks, but enough flexibility to enjoy the spontaneous and creative benefits?

This chapter will explore five major factors that influence collaborative relationships, along with the six broad types of collaborations you are likely to encounter and engage in. But first, let's take one step back to look at what to consider even *before* collaboration.

When to Collaborate

Even with as many benefits as it brings, collaboration will not always be the most effective strategy to meet your goals.

We have already touched briefly on the positives collaborating, but as we will get into more later, joining forces can also present many challenges that need to be navigated. This can be a process so tiring and time-consuming you might wonder why on Earth you thought collaboration was a good idea in the first place!

So before embarking down this road, you have to ask yourself if the potential benefits outweigh the potential challenges. A question whose answer varies with the type of collaborative relationship you enter into - for which there are many forms.

Understanding The Problem

A 2004 article by Ron Heifetz, John Kania and Mark Kramer in the Stanford Social Innovation Review points out the differences between *technical problems* and *adaptive problems*, and how that relates to collaborating for solutions.[2]

Because collaboration can take longer than going it alone, there may be scenarios when it really does make more sense to *not* collaborate.

For example, when the problem is technical, or where it is well-defined and the solution is known, it may be more efficient for just one team or organization to work on delivering that solution to those in need. Heifetz, Kania, and Kramer give examples like better access to higher education or increasing efficiency of a local food bank. They point out that, given the required funding, these issues can be simply resolved by one organization with well-established solutions, like scholarships or inventory control systems.

On the other hand, when the problem is adaptive, or when is it complex and the solution is unknown, collaboration between several partners is more likely to come up with an effective strategy to create lasting change. That is because one organization simply does not have the knowledge or resources to do it alone. The authors' examples of these include reforming public education, restoring wetland environments, and improving community health.

---

[2] *Ronald Heifetz, John Kania, and Mark Kramer, "Leading Boldly", Stanford Social Innovation Review, Winter 2004,* http://ssir.org/articles/entry/leading_boldly

Ask yourself:

> *Is there already a well-known, sound solution for the problem you are tackling?*

If you have the expertise and financial resources you may be better off working on your own than in partnership. (If you don't have the financial means, with the right team you should be able to access resources to implement the solution.)

> *Or is the challenge complex without a clear-cut solution?*

Collaboration or a strategic partnership may be just what you need to start cracking the code.

Since you picked up this book, our guess is you are keen to collaborate!

The 5 Influences of Collaborative Relationships

There are five key factors that influence collaborations:

1. Structure
2. Duration
3. Diversity
4. Leadership
5. Desired Outcomes

Before reaching out and engaging potential partners, you want to consider what type of working relationship you are looking for.

For this, you need a good understanding of where you are at now, what you want to accomplish (where you want to be X time from now) and what type of commitment you are willing to make to get there.

Some collaborative relationships require a high degree of commitment and accountability to function.

16

Others are more loosely structured, and part of the value *they* bring stems from that flexibility. There is not so much a *best way* to collaborate, but there is likely a *best way for you* to collaborate given your preferences and goals.

Thinking through the various types of collaborations and partnerships, there appear to be five major factors that influence what kind of working relationship makes the most sense to form.

After you read through each influence, mark on the spectrum where you feel your 'optimal' collaborative relationship would fall. Note these are not cut and dry, black and white concepts. Most collaborations will end up being a mix of these factors, and absolutely every collaboration will be entirely unique!

INFLUENCE #1 – STRUCTURE

This might not be the first factor you think of when considering various makeups of collaborative partnerships, but it has a huge influence on how partners participate in and engage with the work.

Essentially, this factor looks at how defined or structured the work will be. Will the collaboration be formalized with a written contract or agreement? Or will it be an informal call for collaborators who can come and go as they please or engage when it makes sense for them?

While a highly structured relationship is somewhat self-explanatory, you might be wondering what the opposite side of the spectrum looks like. The opposite of structured collaboration is emergent collaboration, where people are "working with other people towards a common outcome of their own initiative and in a way that is self-guided."[3]

---

[3] *Larry Hawes, "Collaboration Insights Structured vs. Emergent Collaboration Part 1", Dow Brook*

Structure will also impact how well-defined the scope and goals of the project will be. The less structure built into the working relationship, the harder it will be to set and hold partners accountable for meeting those goals. The less structure, the wider the scope of the work because there are fewer agreed-upon parameters to hold the scope of work to a defined edge.

Another element of structure found by the Harvard Business Review is how open or closed participation is within the network.[4] For example, who is invited into the collaboration? Is it open to everyone who wants to join in, or are partners selected based on criteria someone has deemed relevant?

When considering this influence, ask yourself:

> *Is the goal or objective clear, or ambiguous?*
> *What is the minimum that needs to happen to achieve this goal or objective?*
> *How will the work be affected if my partner doesn't follow through on their end of the agreement?*
> *What is more important to me - following a clear plan or leaving room for unexpected changes?*
> *How do I like to work? Is my work style more spontaneous or planned and structured?*
> *Do I need a few specific partners, or several partners from diverse backgrounds, to succeed?*

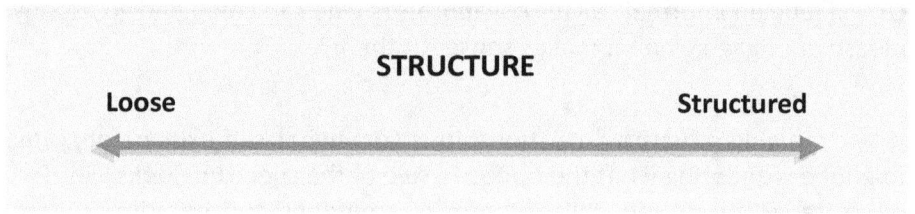

STRUCTURE

Loose   **Structured**

---

[4] *Gary Pisano and Robert Verganti, "Which Kind of Collaboration Is Right for You?", Harvard Business Review, December 2008,*

INFLUENCE # 2 - DURATION

This factor addresses how long the collaborative relationship is expected to last. Collaborations can be formed for one-time events, for short-term projects to achieve time-bound goals, or they can be ongoing long-term commitments with no defined end.

This sense of duration could greatly impact the level of commitment of the partners, and also influence how much attention, thought or intention they bring to the table.

When considering this influence, ask yourself:

> What is the specific goal or objective I am seeking a partner to help me achieve?
> Can it be broken down into smaller objectives?
> Is a partner, or the same partner, needed to achieve all of those objectives?
> If yes, how big/long of a commitment am I willing to make?
> If I am seeking a long-term commitment, what value can I bring to the table, or what gap am I filling for the other partner? ("What's in it for them?")

DURATION

One-time   **Long-term**

<——>

INFLUENCE # 3 - DIVERSITY

This influence looks at how similar or different the partners are who are coming together. Some collaborations will thrive with vast diversity in partners, and others will do better when the partners are carefully selected according to a project's unique set of requirements.

There are probably many elements you could think of that fit into this category, but the two main types of diversity are:

- the size of partners (individuals up to multinational organizations), and
- the depth and/or breadth of expertise they bring into the relationship

As you can imagine, embarking on a collaboration may look quite different between two individuals, two small organizations, two corporations, an individual and a corporation, several individuals, several small organizations, and so on.

When considering this influence, ask yourself:

> What value can a partner of a difference size/level of experience bring to the table that I can't?
> How important is that for accomplishing my goals?
> What downsides are there to working with a partner of that size/experience?
> Is it worth it?

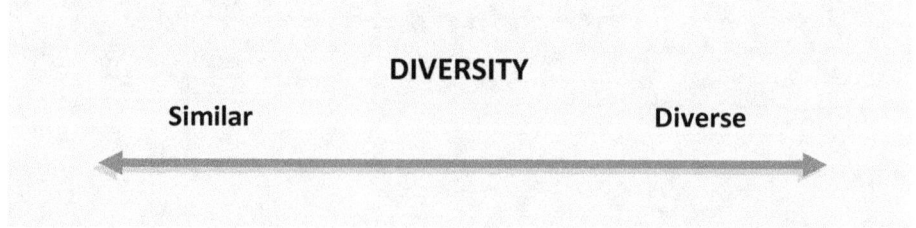

DIVERSITY

Similar   **Diverse**

INFLUENCE # 4 - LEADERSHIP

A collaboration can be organic or purposeful in how it is organized. In large part, what defines how organic or purposeful it is comes down to who is leading and how they chose to lead. The scope of work is also largely influenced by leadership of the collaboration.

Harvard Business Review discusses collaborations having flat or hierarchical governance.[5]

When leadership is flat, the scope of work is determined by the collective. If the collaboration has an open participation structure and flat leadership, the scope of work may never be well-defined.

On the other hand, for a project that is led with hierarchical governance, there is one partner (whether that be an individual or one organization) who primarily decides the scope. In this scenario, you can imagine how when only one partner is articulating the challenge faced, they bring a unique perspective that could greatly influence the proposed the solution, and such, the entire direction of the work.

What's more, if participation is closed and there is a clearly defined leader, the scope of work and desired outcome may not fully represent the complete picture or everyone's motivations.

When considering this influence, ask yourself:

> Is there a leader who has the available 'bandwidth' to lead?
> Does the desired outcome require careful strategy?
> How much could the scope and/or path of work possibly change depending on leadership?
> Is that an issue?

---

[5] *Pisano and Verganti, "Which Kind of Collaboration Is Right for You?"*

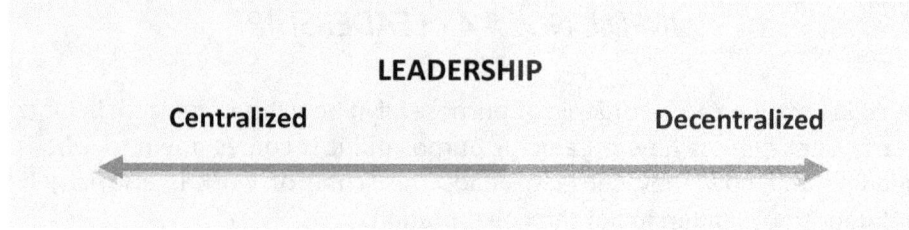

INFLUENCE # 5 - DESIRED OUTCOMES

Methods of collaboration vary with how well-defined the desired goals are. In some cases, there is a very clearly-defined goal.

For example, as in the case of a volunteer team that aims to plan and run a one-time event, it is generally accepted there needs to be a venue, promotion, entertainment, food, and so on.

In other cases, the ultimate goal is unknown at the start. In fact, the goal of a collaborating group could be to come together to share knowledge and use the wisdom of the crowd to determine what their goal *should* be. Some decisions could be made to achieve that goal, but it is far more ambiguous.

Or, maybe there are no specific outcomes from the start and no intention of arriving at any goals!

For example, collaborative Communities of Practice, where participants generally come and go as they please, is not conducive to achieving an ambitious measurable goal.

The strength of this type of collaboration is its flexibility to form to the needs of the participants at any given time. This could not actually be achieved with a clear cut goal.

When considering this influence, ask yourself:

> Is there a defined goal or outcome desired by the partners involved?
> If so, what is it?
> If there is no defined goal, do you want there to be, or is it not necessary?

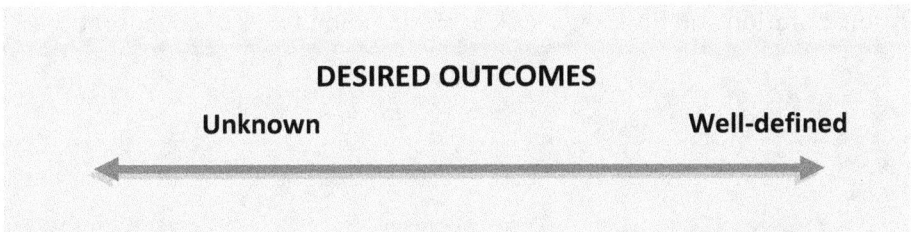

After reflecting on the questions above and reviewing types of collaboration on the following pages, scan the summary table (at the end of the next section) to see what type of collaboration might be the best fit for you and your current goals.

"When minds meet, they don't just exchange facts: they transform, reshape them, draw different implications from them, engage in new trains of thought."

Theodore Zeldin

Types of Collaborations

"Collaborative cultures accelerate the evolution of ideas, because they nurture cross pollination."

David Hodgson

Now that you have a better understanding of the factors that can influence a collaboration and how, let's look at six common types of collaborations.

1. Co-founders
2. Community of Practice
3. Volunteer Teams/Committees
4. Multi-organization Collaborations
5. Joint Ventures
6. Collective Impact

As you review these six types of collaborations, think about how they differ in each of the five influences discussed in the last section. Consider examples from your past where you may have encountered or participated in each type.

What did you like about each? What did you find frustrating? Are there types of collaborations that you prefer to engage in, depending on your working style and personality and preferences?

Remember that no two collaborations are created equal! You may notice that working relationships from your own experiences carry elements from several of these types of collaborative relationships. Some partnerships may have worked better than others, but our guess is you received valuable learning from each that you can now take and apply to the next.

Ok, let's get started!

TYPE # 1 - CO-FOUNDERS

What is it?

Co-founders are a special type of collaboration where two or more individuals come together to navigate the bumpy road of starting a new venture together.

Each co-founder ideally brings a unique set of essential skills to the team, and each co-founder carries a high level of responsibility for the success of the company.

Even in cases where one person takes charge as the leader, co-founders all work tirelessly together to create value where it didn't exist before. In exchange, they each take partial ownership of the venture in hopes their efforts will pay off in the long run (in a variety of ways, such as financial or reputational) as the venture thrives.

Example

Bureo Skateboards[6] is a successful social business that was founded by a team of three surfer environmentalists.

Bureo has a plastic fishnet recycling program to reduce ocean plastic waste and uses this recycled material in lifestyle products like their original skateboard, and sunglasses.

Alone we can do so little; together we can do so much.
Helen Keller

---

[6] *Bureo Skateboards, http://bureo.co/team.php*

TYPE # 2 - COMMUNITY OF PRACTICE

What is it?

Pioneers in social learning, Etienne and Beverly Wenger-Trayner[7], describe Communities of Practice (CoPs) as: "groups of people who share a concern or a passion for something they do and learn how to do it better as they interact regularly."

Communities of Practice come in many forms but share a specific set of defining factors. CoPs are different than other networks because they are formed specifically around a 'domain' of expertise. This domain could be a particular profession, industry, or subject of interest, such as social entrepreneurship.

Another defining factor is that CoPs are comprised of members who meet to discuss, problem-solve and share ideas related to their interest domain.

As Etienne and Beverly Wenger-Trayner describe, the final factor in CoPs is, "a shared repertoire of resources: experiences, stories, tools, ways of addressing recurring problems—in short a shared practice."

Example

Does this type of collaboration sound familiar? This is the type of collaborative community we have been actively creating within the Global Social Entrepreneurs Lab![8]

There are several similar examples of online or in-person groups and communities where members jump in and engage when they can and when it works for them.

---

[7] Etienne and Beverly Wenger-Trayner, "Introduction to communities of practice", http://wenger-trayner.com/introduction-to-communities-of-practice/

[8] The Global Social Entrepreneur's Lab, http://globalsocentlab.com/

There is no defined work, or goal, but members receive great benefit accessing support from their peers and the opportunity to bounce ideas and collect feedback.

"Social innovation thrives on collaboration; on doing things with others, rather than just to them or for them: hence the great interest in new ways of using the web to 'crowdsource' ideas, or the many experiments involving users in designing services."

Geoff Mulgan

TYPE # 3 – VOLUNTEER TEAMS/COMMITTEES

What is it?

This type of collaboration is pretty straight-forward, and our guess is you have already experienced it at one time or another! If you have ever joined forces with a small team to plan a fundraiser event, sat on a volunteer board for a local nonprofit, or contributed your expertise to a volunteer working group, then you have the idea.

This type of collaboration is simple in that it doesn't usually require long lead time, or investment setting a foundation before individuals can get on board. If an existing committee, project or organization is seeking volunteers, in the best of situations there may be an intake process, but when a competent prospective volunteer is interested in helping there is little barrier to doing so.

That said, these collaborations can also be tricky in that they are usually project-based, and not always a priority of those involved (since it is often time dedicated on top of life's many other pressing priorities).

Example

Several nonprofits and charities grow their impact through local volunteer chapters. One example is Acumen, a global nonprofit that invests in businesses who are scaling innovations that provide critical goods and services to those living in poverty.

Acumen has been generating consistently impressive impact with a small staff team. One way they expand their reach is through local volunteer-led chapters in roughly 30 cities around the world.

These self-managed local chapters recruit and organize a volunteer committee that works to raise capital and awareness for Acumen's global efforts, and to connect people and ideas in the social impact space.

"Those that regularly come into contact with people having diverse interests and viewpoints are more likely to come up with innovative ideas."

Steven Johnson

TYPE # 4 - MULTI-ORGANIZATION COLLABORATIONS

What is it?

Again, there is an incredible variety in how this type of collaboration will take shape. It could be a partnership between two or more organizations to develop a unique service or offering.

Or, it could be a multi-stakeholder group of people wanting to get an idea into their community that requires more hands-on-deck to implement it well.

Example

One example of a multi-stakeholder community-wide collaboration is AlbertaIN.[9] In response to the lack of a clear pathway for entrepreneurs to follow when seeking services for launching and funding new companies, the goal of this project was to better connect organizations in Alberta, Canada, who serve entrepreneurs.

Through several conversations and a few large roundtable meetings, Alberta Innovates acted as a champion to bring the community together.

Now that AlbertaIN exists, organizations across the province have a better understanding of both what else is available, and when to refer entrepreneurs to the right service providers.

"In an increasingly connected world it is less likely that a few people 'manage' everyone else. The new environment requires a shift in the organization of both institutions and societies, one of flexible teams of teams that come together around whatever change opportunities exist and then reform around the next."

Bill Drayton, Ashoka

TYPE # 5 - JOINT VENTURES

What is it?

A Joint Venture is a long-term collaboration where two or more partners come together and agree to jointly form a brand new legal company that is (usually) equally owned by the partners.

---

[9] *AlbertaIN, http://www.albertain.com/*

Example

Yunus, with his social business model to fight poverty, and Riboud, with his expertise in food products, joined forces to produce a new type of yogurt - one that has critical nutrients and is also affordable, even to the poorest of the poor. In addition to developing a product that delivers needed nutrition at a reasonable price point, the joint venture is a true social business, where with every decision, social and environmental impact are top of mind.

See chapter 7 for more details on Joint Ventures in action.

TYPE # 6 - COLLECTIVE IMPACT

What is it?

Collective Impact Initiatives are a unique type of collaboration where many organizations (in some cases hundreds) come together to align themselves with shared goals and objectives within a complex social challenge, such as education or community health.

This type of collaboration is complex and requires a long-term time commitment from everyone involved. It also requires a dedicated "backbone" organization or steering committee to guide the process in order for it to be successful.

Given the need for a central organization or committee and the long timeline of collaboration, it can be challenging to find financial support for a collective impact initiative to take form.

However, recent success in projects, such as transforming education in the United States, provides great learning and hope for this type of collaboration to continue succeeding in the future in the world of social change.

> *"The urge to form partnerships, to link up in a collaborative arrangement, is perhaps the oldest, strongest, and most fundamental force in nature. There are no solitary, free-living creatures: every form of life is dependent on other forms."*
>
> **Lewis Thomas**

Example

Strive is a collective impact initiative that brought together 300 public and private organizations to improve the educational system in Cincinnati. With their collective sights set on improving a 53 education success factors, Strive has improved 64% of them, including high school graduation rates, fourth-grade reading and math scores, and the number of preschool children prepared for kindergarten.[10]

See Chapter 7 for more detail on Collective Impact in action, including a case study.

*Note: Both Joint Ventures and Collective Impact are discussed in more detail in **Chapter 7 - Looking Towards Collaboration on a Larger Scale.***

> *"The ability and desire to transform the mundane materials at hand that we both bring into the collaboration well beyond the sum total of the parts - to birth a new baby neither of us could claim single parentage of."*
>
> **Gary Lucas**

---

[10] *John Kania and Mark Kramer, "Collective Impact", Stanford Social Innovation Review, http://ssir.org/articles/entry/collective_impact*

Types of Collaborations summary table

	Structure	Duration
Co-founders	Closed and structured	Long-term
Volunteer Teams/ Committees	Open participation but structured	Can be time-bound (project-based) or long-term commitments
Communities of Practice	Open and unstructured	Long-term
Multi-organization collaboration	Closed (chosen) and Structured	Any duration
Collective Impact	Structured	Long-term
Joint Ventures	Structured	Long-term

Diversity of Partners	Leadership	Desired Outcomes
Individuals with complementary experience/ skills	Decentralized between only a few people (~2-4)	Usually clearly defined
Similar (individuals)	Usually centralized, i.e. committee chair	Clearly defined goals and outcomes
Varies (engagement is individual)	Decentralized, no leadership	No tangible goals or outcomes
Similar (organizations, but size can vary)	Varies	Defined
Varies (individuals and organizations)	Centralized (backbone organization)	Clearly defined
Similar (organizations, but partners could vary in size)	Varies	Varies

CHAPTER 2

Collaboration Roadmap

CHAPTER 2 - COLLABORATION ROADMAP

The Nuts and Bolts of Practical Application!

"Collaboration is the best way to work. It's the only way to work, really. Everyone's there because they have a set of skills to offer across the board."

Antony Starr

Now that you made it this far in this book, you understand *why* collaborations are important to grow your social impact. In this chapter, we'll look at *how* to make them happen!

Collaborations are important because, not only will it be more enjoyable for you as an individual, but it is a great way for you to contribute to changing the world for the better. Isn't this why we all became changemakers? To do something bigger than ourselves, and to help make the world a better place?

From this broad vision, let's have a look at the actual steps and see how it can be made into reality.

Like any business strategy, there is a step-by-step process you can follow in order to maximize the opportunity to grow sustainable collaborations and partnerships.

There are 4 keys to drive (lean) collaborations.

Step 1 - Get Clarity
Step 2 - Reach Out
Step 3 - Seal the Deal
Step 4 - Drive It Forward (or Not!)

For each step, we will look at two types of collaboration:

- <u>Internal Collaborations</u>:
  People collaborating within your organization, for example as a co-founder or a key contributor, etc.

- <u>External Collaborations</u>:
  Collaborating with an external existing initiative, for example on a side-project, or for one aspect of your activities.

For each collaboration type, we will take a "lean" approach.

Meaning, instead of working to make something 100% perfect from the beginning (which takes a lot of time and energy, and doesn't necessarily provide the best results), we'll give space for the collaboration to grow little by little into a sustainable partnership.

Practical Example

Traditionally, an entrepreneur would hire a full-time web designer as an employee once the enterprise budget allows it. The "lean" version would be to outsource a few web design tasks to a potential web designer via short-term, project contracts earlier on.

The commitment and investment could then grow gradually, with flexibility to grow into something more permanent like an employer/employee relationship, or more dynamic like a co-founder relationship.

Why go "lean" for your collaborations? Because it is less risky, more affordable and more scalable over the long run. Plus, it fits with the overall values of social innovation: trust, creativity, individual initiative, and having a long-term outlook.

Ok, ready? It's time to take action!

Step # 1 - Get Clarity

Before reaching out to anyone, or jumping to say "yes!" on any invitation to collaborate, a very important step is to get clear on what you really want, what you really need, and why.

Just like you did not start your social enterprise based on the very first idea that crossed your mind, don't go ahead with the first collaboration idea that shows up.

> First, it will be hard for you to be convincing as a strong collaborator without a clear scope and strong vision for where you'd like to go with a partner.

> Second, in the event the collaboration starts it will most likely be a waste of time (and sometimes money) for all involved if you are not aligned with a vision for how the collaboration will work, or on the mission for what you want to accomplish together.

Let's now look at *how* to get clarity before starting a collaboration.

The first step is to decide on *one* key problem, or gap, that you hope the collaboration can fill.

> Is it a skill gap?
> Is it a reputation, or legitimacy problem?
> Is it a visibility issue? (not attracting enough demand)
> Is it a capacity struggle? (attracting too much demand)
> Is it a growth challenge?

In many cases, your ideal collaboration will contribute to several aspects of your social business. However, it is important to have one primary focus to lead it forward.

Now, let's look at practical applications for both internal and external collaborations.

38

For Internal Collaborations:

Before searching for the specific individual who you would want to work with, ask yourself if you need someone to primarily...

... do something you do not know how to do yourself?
... bring a network, and become the face of your enterprise?
... bring sales and marketing knowledge and experience, to allow your enterprise to be financially sustainable?
... increase the capacity of your work, locally or in another region?
.. contribute to something else?

Being clear on *why* you need an extra collaborator, or a co-founder, is what will allow you to find the right partner. You will not only be able to communicate more clearly with potential candidates, but you will be also better equipped to recognize an opportunity when it is presented to you.

For External Collaborations:

Before searching for a particular initiative that you want to work with, ask yourself if you need a collaborator to primarily...

...fill a skill gap, or enter a market/location where you have little to no experience?
... make your own solution more legitimate to increase its reach and impact?
... increase your capacity to handle the demand?
... contribute something else?

Again, a collaboration with another partner can bring extra skills, legitimacy, or capacity, etc. to your initiative, but knowing what you want most will help you select the best fit. This will allow for your impact to reach its full potential!

Maybe you noticed that none of the examples above mention money or material goods.

The reason is that true collaborations must be more than just an exchange of money. Sharing physical, tangible goods is one thing, but sharing a goal, a vision and a passion are what will make your collaborations truly fruitful.

> *"If you have an apple and I have an apple and we exchange these apples then you and I will still each have one apple. But if you have an idea and I have an idea and we exchange these ideas, then each of us will have two ideas."*
>
> **George Bernard Shaw**

All clear on why you want to partner with someone or another initiative? Time for Step 2!

Step # 2 - Reach Out

This step doesn't start with taking out your phone out and reaching out to potential partners. Why? Because you don't even know yet who to reach out to yet!

Identify Potential Partners

> *Use people whom you're excited by and who share your excitement... The ideal collaboration is one in which the actor and director are saying to each other, 'I can't believe how lucky we are to be making a movie together.'*
>
> **James Toback**

Now that you know *why* you want to collaborate, it is time to list *who* you want to collaborate with. And by 'who' we mean real human beings!

With social media, it is easy to identify a number of people who could fit the 'ideal collaborator' you are looking for. Look around! LinkedIn and Twitter are perfect tools for this task.

You can sort out people depending on your criteria.

For Internal Collaborations:

- Look for people who have the interest, title, and experience you need.

For External Collaborations:

- List the entities you DREAM to collaborate with.
- Identify the title of the person who would be the decision-maker (CEO? Marketing Manager? CSR Manager?).
- Find out who that is in the organizations you have selected.

Plant the seeds

Now, should you go ahead and contact them about your partnership idea? Nope, still not yet!

Would you say "yes" to someone you have never met before if they asked you to marry them in a LinkedIn, twitter or Facebook message? Probably not. In fact, you would probably disregard them altogether or you might even report them to the social media platform for harassment. Why? Because the relationship is not built yet!

Collaboration is like marriage: you cannot propose on the first encounter. You haven't even started dating yet! At this time you are not at the 'pitch your idea' phase, you are at the 'start the relationship' phase.

What you can do is to start planting seeds. Seeds are small. They are simple. They are not enough to harvest big fruits, but this is where it all starts.

For every potential partner, you should (at least!):

> Follow their twitter account.
> "Like" their professional Facebook page (ideally with your professional Facebook page).
> Invite them to join your LinkedIn network (with a tailor-made message).

Water Your Plants

Seeding can be done all at once. Watering seeds requires more patience (and too much water actually kills the plant, so don't take the risk of sounding pushy; take your time).

The idea is not only to get noticed but also to get to know them. What do they care about? What challenges do they seem to face? What gaps do they have that you might be able to help fill?

Here is how to nurture the relationship until you get noticed:

> Join the groups your potential collaborators are part of and share your work (articles, events, etc) roughly once a week
> Comment on their posts in their most active social media channels
> Share their posts on your social media accounts (and mention them in the posts)
> Mention them in your blog posts when it makes sense, and share the article with them via email
> Promote their offer/events/news to your own network
> Go to events they organize (if applicable)
> Answer their newsletter (if applicable) to let them know what you think about their work, or to say what they do is really inspiring!

In one word: generosity. GIVE before you receive.

Using this 'lean' way of getting to know each other will also help you validate they are not only good candidates on paper, but also fit with your values and vision.

During this phase, short-list your top ideal collaborators.

Harvest

Once you have been in touch for a while (which you can do simultaneously with different potential partners), you can take the first step and invite them to collaborate.

For potential partnerships where you have already started your own initiative:

> You can:
> - Interview them and feature their initiative in your blog or in your network,
> - Invite them to speak at one of your events,
> - Invite them to co-host an event with you.

For reaching out to potential co-founders:

If you have not yet started any of the above (blogging, organizing events) you can contact them and invite to a coffee or brainstorming session.

Your arguments?

- Explain you are soon launching an initiative in XYZ sector,
- you want to gather a small crowd of people doing great work in this field,
- you have noticed them on social media or in your community,
- and you think they might be interested in your project.

Once again, this step will help you trim down the number of potential partners. If you have 'watered your plants' correctly, this step should go really well!

Keep in mind, those who are not open to collaborating at this point are probably not the people you will want to collaborate with. At least not at this point in your journey. If you did your homework to understand their point-of-view, then started an open conversation and still found they weren't receptive to a small collaboration, what are the chances it would work on a larger scale?

In summary, and as you can see, at this point you are still far from co-creating and collaborating in the long run together. Still, this is where it starts!

You won't get married on a first date, right? So don't hope to "hack" the relationship. Trust the process if you want to build sustainable, fruitful collaborations.

If this first interaction goes well, then you can make the magic grow!

Make It Grow

This first interaction is like a pilot project. You can test out anything you want!

Carefully Ask Yourself

> Do you like the other person's work style?
> Do you trust him/her to build a collaboration together?
> Does he/she still seem like the perfect fit for the gap you had identified when initiating your partnership plan?

Once you have answered these questions, go ahead and share your idea! Ask if they would like to collaborate with you on a small project, and also, be open to their suggestions. Your collaboration idea will likely evolve into something new as different perspectives come into play.

Many ideas grow better when transplanted into another mind than the one where they sprang up.

Oliver Wendell Holmes

If you are not sure who your ideal collaborative partner is, you can use the Q&A tool we have prepared for you in the Bonus Resource section at the end of the book.

Step # 3 - Seal the Deal

Discuss Scope, Roles, and Timelines

Congratulations on finding your dream partner! Now, you need to secure your partnership by sealing the deal.

"Collaboration happens when the right players share a strong sweet spot of mutual interest, and agree on an apt collaboration method and rules of engagement."

Kare Anderson

In order to come to an agreement, you will need to define the scope of your initiative together, including who does what and when.

Don't aim for the moon to reach a star. Be down to earth, and agree on a scope that is feasible, at least for a start. Your collaboration may lead to a lifelong, large-scale initiative, sure, but you are not quite there yet!

A 'lean' way to map out the scope of your work together is to start with a one-year timeline. Later, after the first year, you can draft a longer vision (maybe 5-years). By then you will have many more elements to add in and a much better understanding of the work.

Here are some key questions you should answer with your partner:

> What are you going to create together?
> What is your overall goal in terms of impact?
> What is your overall goal in terms of revenue?
> Who will be in charge of what tasks?
> How much time and money will each partner invest into the initiative?
> What are the 3 to 5 big steps you will take together over the coming year?

See the Bonus Resource section for an overview of how to use the GROW framework as a tool for goal setting. GROW stands for Goal, Reality, Options/ Obstacles, Way Forward, and is a fantastic way to make sure you don't forget anything.

Depending on the type of collaboration, you might want to also draft an official agreement.

For Internal Collaborations:
- With a co-founder, you can either not sign anything at the start, or you can complete a Memorandum of Understanding
- With a collaborator, and especially if he or she will be on your payroll, you can draft an employment contract according to the guidelines of your jurisdiction.

For External Collaborations:
- If you are dealing with a partner of roughly the same size, you can either not sign anything at the start (especially if this is a small scope partnership for which you will dedicate less than 50% of your time), or you can complete a Memorandum of Understanding (ideal if you will be dedicating more than 50% of your time and/or resources to this partnership)
- If you are dealing with a much smaller or larger partner, you should draft a written agreement. A Memorandum of Understanding is a good format to adopt for this purpose.

Definition of Memorandum of Understanding (MoU) [11]

"Describes a bilateral or multilateral agreement between two or more parties. It expresses a convergence of will between the parties, indicating an intended common line of action.

Whether or not a document constitutes a binding contract depends only on the presence or absence of well-defined legal elements in the text proper of the document (the so-called "four corners"). The required elements are: offer and acceptance, consideration, and the intention to be legally bound (animus contrahendi)."

Be sure to check the specifics of what to include as per your jurisdiction. If you decide not to sign a Memorandum of Understanding, it is best to have a written action plan that all partners have agreed to, to make sure everyone is on the same page.

Sealing the deal, in the form of a Memorandum of Understanding or not, is a small step of the collaborative process. However, it is important as it sets a strong foundation upon which the collaboration can thrive and go forward with as little misunderstanding as possible.

You are now ready to move forward onto the fourth and last step of the process!

---

[11] *Wikipedia, "Memorandum of Understanding",*
https://en.wikipedia.org/wiki/Memorandum_of_understanding

Step # 4 - Drive It Forward (or Not!)

"For productive collaboration adopt five principles: involve the relevant stakeholders, build consensus phase by phase, design a process map, designate a process facilitator and harness the power of group memory."

David Straus and Thomas C. Layton

- Relevant stakeholder: *check!*
- Consensus: *check!*
- Process map: *to check,*
- Process facilitation: *to check,*
- Power of the group: *to monitor along the way!*

In this fourth and last part, we will look at how to map out, facilitate, and measure the success of your partnership.

Outline and Check In on Key Milestones

It is important to agree on the scope and overall vision, but also, on the steps you will take together to get there. Why? Because while you may agree on where to go, there are tons of ways to get there.

Your vision is shaped by your experience and this impacts what you see as the best path forward. Your partner's vision is shaped by his or her own experience and he or she may see a different way forward.

Keep in mind, you don't need to share everything 50/50. Ideally, all partners involved will get to do things they love and are great at, as well as few things they are less enthusiastic about. Sometimes work divides up pretty easily and sometimes it requires a longer discussion to make sure everyone is both happy with their workload and does not feel left out.

Be sure to always plan these three elements ahead of time:

1 - Major steps (or milestones),
2 - Deadlines,
3 - Who is doing what.

For example, when co-writing this book, we agreed on the following plan.

Step 1	Agree on a theme for the book	December 2016	Danielle & Solène
Step 2	Write an outline of the chapters and find key references	December 2016	Danielle
Step 3	Divide chapters between 2 writers + define a target page count for each section	December 2016	Solène
Step 4	Write the content + bonuses + get testimonials from social entrepreneurs	January 2016 / February 2016	Danielle & Solène, each on their own
Step 5	Proofread everything, and make it fit together	March 2016	Danielle
Step 6	Design everything to be easy to read & fit with publishing guidelines	March 2016	Solène
Step 7	Find & validate the title	March 2016	Danielle
Step 8	Design the cover	March 2016	Solène
Step 9	Publish (figure out technical aspect and set up payment)	March 2016	Solène
Step 10	Launch & Promote	March 2016/April 2016	Danielle & Solène

Once your collaboration plan is outlined, you can get to work!

In chapter 6 we will discuss best practices to focus on, and pitfalls to avoid, while driving your collaborations forward. But first, let's close this fourth step by looking at how to measure your success, and what to do if it is not successful.

Measures of Success

How will you know if the partnership has been a success?

This step is similar to assessing the impact of your work in general. Select Key Performance Indicators (KPI) and for each find an element to measure for your assessment.

If we continue with our book example, a quantitative KPI could be the number of books sold. A qualitative KPI could be the number of positive comments on Amazon.

Our actual impact goal is for many social entrepreneurs to improve the way they collaborate and thus scale their impact. But this cannot be easily measured, so it is not considered a KPI.

A collaboration is not just about the impact created, it is also about the human adventure around it! A commonly used KPI is: do both collaborators want to continue working together? And if yes, on what?

Exit Strategies

Just like any human adventure, a collaboration can go bad. Sometimes one of the partners cannot continue for any number of reasons, from personal reasons, to an accident, or simply may not want to continue.

Ideally, your exit strategy will be outlined in the Memorandum of Understanding, or your initial written agreement.

Here are the key questions that should be answered:

> If one partner decides not to continue, how much notice should be given before exiting the partnership, in order for a smooth transition? (i.e. 1 month? 3 months?)
> Who is responsible for finding a replacement? The one who leaves or the one who stays?
> How will you handle a case of a conflict over who gets to continue on alone with the project?

Although these are not easy questions to answer when you get started, just like a prenuptial, it can make things so much easier during a separation.

Because a collaboration is not about feelings (like a wedding is) but is about doing business together, we strongly advise you to get those questions answered (especially if most of your personal income relies on the partnership).

In summary, collaboration is great. Monitored collaboration is better!

You are strategic about your social enterprise. You have probably written a business plan and maybe even joined an accelerator program in order to maximize your chances to be successful.

Imagine the impact your collaborations will have if you are as strategic with them as you are with your social enterprise as a whole!

CHAPTER 3

Case Study: The Global Social Entrepreneurs Lab

CHAPTER 3 - CASE STUDY: THE GLOBAL SOCIAL ENTREPRENEURS LAB

A Story of Aligned Action to Give Social Entrepreneurs the Tools and Community They Need to Grow Impact

As you may know by now, the collaboration between Creators for Good and the Sedge has been growing and evolving since 2014. Since we have found so much success with our collaboration, we wanted to take the time to reflect on how it evolved and what factors were critical to its success.

Setting the Stage

Enter mid-2013...

Along with two team members at the time, Danielle founded theSedge.org with a vision for connecting social entrepreneurs around the world together to share in learning, best practice, and mutual support. The community model grew into online education with the launch of BOOST Academy, where social entrepreneurs could learn the skills they needed to grow an impactful social enterprise.

Now onto mid-2014...

Solène launched Creators for Good, a consulting service for value-driven individuals around the world transitioning from successful-yet-unfulfilling careers to create their own profitable and impactful businesses.

As all inquisitive new founders do, Solène researched the 'competition' in the space and came across the Sedge.

Solène reached out to Danielle a few months after launching Creators for Good. She was not having the social impact that she hoped for, found herself struggling to compete with free initiatives, and started wondering if it was even possible to be financially sustainable in this field...

Now, at this time the Sedge had been through some growing pains itself, trying to innovate an impactful and financially sustainable online model to connect social entrepreneurs around the world to exchange ideas, best practices, and grow the confidence they needed to charge forward with their socially entrepreneurial goals.

Danielle was grateful to connect with a fellow social entrepreneurship coach whose passion was helping smart visionary changemakers launch successful social enterprises.

Getting to Know Each Other

When Solène reached out to Danielle, she did so in a very authentic way, explaining the challenges and asking to hear about her experience.

Both holding the view that there is no 'competition' in the social enterprise world, we realized that we shared very similar values and vision for the change we wanted to create in the world - empowering social entrepreneurs.

Beginning an Informal Collaboration

When Danielle was brainstorming what might be fun for her community, she thought of Solène and reached back out to see if she wanted to join forces for a live Q&A event.

We brainstormed a few names for our event and landed on the Live #Socent Lab - Collaborative Q&A for social entrepreneurs. We drafted a quick survey to share with our communities to help pick our topic, and the first event was held on June 2nd, 2015 on the (very fitting) topic of Collaborations and Partnerships.

Growing

At the first Q&A, the response from participants was overwhelmingly positive! People were asking how they could stay connected after the call.

We were very much following the demand from our first live call together and decided to extend the collaboration through co-hosting a Facebook group. And so the Global Social Entrepreneurs Lab Facebook Group was born.

It was another low-risk, low-investment project to take on together. Again, we were remaining flexible and adaptable.

We truly both enjoyed co-hosting the first Live #Socent Q&A, and it was met with such a warm welcome from both our communities that we knew we wanted to keep the learning opportunities flowing.

We decided to co-host (roughly) quarterly Q&A calls under the same brand we had already created together.

The next three calls were on:
- Market Validation
- Planning an Impactful 2016
- Marketing & Communication

Formalizing a Partnership

Near the end of 2015, the Global Social Entrepreneurs Lab had grown to 300 members and was growing organically every day. At this time, it became apparent to both Solène and Danielle that there was an opportunity in each of our businesses to take more targeted steps to foster and strategically grow what began so organically.

The next phase of our collaboration was to plan and implement a more structured partnership. This phase included creating this book, and introducing a new offering to our members of the Global Social Entrepreneurs Lab, a paid membership learning community for social entrepreneurs around the world.

Reflecting on Key Success Factors

So why exactly did this loose-collaboration turned structured-partnership work so well? What was it about the external environment, our own mindsets, and the internal factors in each of our businesses that allowed this relationship to thrive?

Individual Visions that Were Aligned Before We Even Started

One of the most critical factors above all was that we both shared a vision for change. The Sedge and Creators for Good share a mission of helping social entrepreneurs succeed and grow thriving social enterprises that have an impact while being financially sustainable.

Not only that, but we shared a very similar target audience of globally aware changemakers who feel compelled to make a difference in the world. Although the Sedge and Creators for Good are so aligned in mission, the interesting thing is that we chose very different paths to achieve that goal. Solène chose to deliver high-touch one-on-one consulting services, and Danielle chose to create wider-reaching but less personalized online courses.

It was a natural fit to work together because people in each of our audiences may have found the other offering to be better suited to their needs, thus helping get the right solution in front of those who needed it.

Both Coming from a Position of Strength

When we first started working together, there was very little risk. We did not enter the relationship as a 'hail mary' to save our businesses; neither of us was sinking and reaching out for a life raft. It was a low-risk collaboration, which also meant low-reward.

But that was ok because we were each solid on our own, and the collaboration was a 'nice-to-have' experiment, not a 'must-have'.

With both of us coming from a position of strength, there was little chance for misrepresenting our motives or expectations for the collaboration. It also allowed us to each show up fully and represent ourselves and our ideas from a very authentic place.

Started Small and Grew Collaboration Over Time

Initially, we never set out to build a formal partnership. Instead, it grew gradually over time. We started small with a one-time informal online event, and at each step along the way were able to decide if and how we each wanted to move the working relationship forward.

Open and Clear Communication

This is so crucial for anyone collaborating. Practicing open and clear communication is essential for navigating misunderstandings, assumptions, and expectations throughout the process. Imagine trying to arrive in the same town as your partner without knowing the town's name or having the same directions! In any project, it is inevitable that there will be differing preferences or points-of-view on how to move forward towards the goal, or how to solve unexpected challenges. At these times especially, all parties need to feel comfortable and confident communicating their point of view in a constructive way.

Luckily, in the case of the Global Social Entrepreneurs Lab, there haven't been any major disagreements at this point. But we have both been confident to share our new ideas and any suggestions for improvements along the way, knowing our opinions will be heard and respected.

Complementary Work Styles

Not everyone will have working styles that complement each other. If that is the case, it could cause significant challenges in a collaboration. One example is a threshold for deadlines. Some people thrive setting short, ambitious deadlines, but for others that could bring up overwhelming feelings of anxiety or stress.

As it turns out, we have very complementary work styles. We both value planning tasks and deadlines, are motivated to follow through, and are comfortable taking initiative moving tasks forward without necessarily checking in on every detail. This comfort in working independently is a result of last two key success factors.

Shared Vision for the Outputs and Outcomes of the Collaborative Work Itself

After working together on a few tasks, we quickly realized that not only were our work styles complementary, but we had a similar vision for the type of work we wanted to create.

Our thresholds for attention to detail and overall quality seemed to be calibrated at similar levels. We also shared the same vision for what we were aiming to achieve through our collaborative efforts.

Reliability and Trust Built Early On

Again, by starting small and growing over time, we were able to build greater trust and reliability with every step.

We checked in with each other on several decisions early on, but with every new decision where we realized we were 'on the same page', we gained greater trust in the other to execute to the standard, quality, and style we both held ourselves to.

Now that you have read the 'behind the scenes' of our own successful collaboration, it is time to also share with you the other face of the coin: the pitfalls that need to be avoided to grow such a partnership!

CHAPTER 4

The 6 Most Common Collaboration Pitfalls

CHAPTER 4 -
THE 6 MOST COMMON
COLLABORATION PITFALLS

And How to Avoid or Solve Them

So far, we have primarily looked at the bright side of collaboration. By now you understand *why* collaboration is worth pursuing and *how* to best approach it following the Collaboration Roadmap.

However, with every opportunity comes a risk!

How many social enterprise projects have failed, not because the idea was bad or unsustainable, but because the team did not stick together long enough to make it happen?

Obviously, we don't want that to happen to you... Hence this book, and this chapter!

As social entrepreneurs, our job is to bring innovative ideas to life. To contribute to making the world a better place. It is *also* our job to come up with the best strategies and managerial practices in order for our world-changing ideas to last and actually transform our societies!

With this chapter, you will not only learn what potential collaboration pitfalls to avoid but also *how* to avoid and/or solve them.

The 6 Most Common Collaboration Pitfalls are the following:

While Starting the Collaboration:
1. Collaborating "Just Because"
2. Misalignment of Goals
3. Lack of Direction or Leadership

While Growing the Collaboration:
4. Miscommunication and Misunderstandings
5. Clashing Work Styles
6. Lack of Formalization

Pitfall #1 - Collaborating "Just Because"

Collaboration is about joining forces and complementing each other. It is not about feeling less lonely or looking good on the outside.

If you are looking for a co-founder, be clear on the skills you want he or she to bring to the table. It should not "just" be about motivating you!

If you are looking for an existing organization to collaborate with, think about what you bring to the table, and not just what you have to gain (like press coverage!).

Example

T. is happy. He has now validated his social business idea! He is still quite shy to talk about the details (what if someone hears about it and starts it before him?!).

He often goes to networking events and inspiring conferences where he meets tons of like-minded entrepreneurs. One day, a contact puts him in touch with a friend who also wants to launch a social business. After only one meeting, they decide they will partner up!

Of course, T. has to compromise on his original idea to include his new co-founder's input. That's part of the game!

They find a name they both like, work hard to build the content of their offer, and start building their website. As the launch deadline approaches, they realize they need more time to integrate all the ideas that are showing up along the way.

However, three months later nothing is ready. Simple became complicated, making even the smallest decisions is taking much longer than expected, and compromising on the compromises means that neither co-founder is feeling fully committed to moving forward.

T. starts to lose his patience, and his bank account starts to go dry. One fight later, he is told he will have to continue alone. This failed collaboration is one of the first experiences of his entrepreneurial journey, before even launching his social business.

The project as it is now doesn't "sound like him". He decides to stop everything, goes back to start over with his initial idea, and launches a month later.

Two years have passed and T. is still running his initiative. He now has two people working full time with him. These people are committed to driving his initiative further, and are not collaborating "just because".

Ask Yourself

> What skills do you lack, that your ideal collaborator should have to help drive your initiative forward?

Take Action
In order to avoid this pitfall, we challenge you to:

> *Work on your own value proposition before inviting or accepting collaborators into your project. The more solid YOU are, the more solid collaborations will be in contributing to your impact.*

Pitfall #2 - Misalignment of Goals

Having a shared vision is the most important of all; no one can work together if looking in different directions.

> The secret is to gang up on the problem, rather than each other.
>
> **Thomas Stallkamp**

Example
J. is a marketer who is passionate about social innovation. She worked for a few years in a company that distributes monthly ethical gift boxes. One day, she meets M., a nutritionist working a revolutionary project. The project helps seniors adapt their diet (and get the vitamins and nutrients they need to prevent Alzheimer's and other common gerontology-related illnesses) while remaining independent from nursing homes. Together, J. and M. have an idea - why not offer a weekly food box tailor-made for seniors?

J. is not as passionate as M. about the 'silver economy' (products and services adapted for the elderly), but she is delighted to use her delivery box business model expertise and logistics skills for a project close to her social innovation values. Plus, she likes the idea of developing her own initiative where she can have more freedom than in her current job. She looks forward to being free to take part in more initiatives, and as a single mom, to be free to spend more time with her son and daughter. She quits her job, and dedicates 100% of her time to the new project!

J. and M. partner up and start a one-year mentoring program to develop and launch their idea. The methodology of their incubation center is quite strict; they have to prototype their solution before launching anything. Throughout the market research, J. and M. realize the potential beneficiaries do not want to get food delivered to their house because grocery shopping is one of the few opportunities they have to socialize.

The business model shifts into a nutrition center where the elderly can shop from local farms and take advantage of help from dieticians to plan healthy and nutritious meals.

J. cannot use her expertise anymore, and does not feel like dedicating that much time and energy into a project she's less motivated about. Plus, opening a physical place means bigger investment to be held responsible for, working during the weekend, etc. J. doesn't want to commit anymore. M. has to look for a new partner, or the incubation center might revoke her from the mentorship program. J. decides to launch her own food box, this time for single moms!

Long story short, and as the saying goes, "fall in love with the problem, be flexible about the solution!"

Ask Yourself

> What is your overall vision? Where do you see your initiative in 5 years?

Take Action
In order to avoid this pitfall, we challenge you to:

> *Share your vision with your potential and existing partners. Make sure they are flexible about the path you may take to achieve a clear vision you all agree on.*

Pitfall #3 - Miscommunication and Misunderstandings

One key to fruitful collaboration is healthy communication.

> *"Assumptions are the termites of relationships."*
>
> ***Henry Winkler***

Lack of communication, or misleading communication, can easily lead to misunderstanding. If partners take action without fully understanding each other's expectations, it can lead to wasted time, duplication of work, and unnecessary tensions.

Example
FC. and KV. are two organizations in the field of innovative personal development. One day, the co-founders of FC. (F. and C.) offer to interview K., the founder of KV, for their blog. This interview is an occasion for everyone to get to know each other.

One day, K. comes up with an idea. Why not join forces and organize the first Happiness Innovation Day, an annual event where speakers, researchers, entrepreneurs and key organizations in this field would come together and share their perspectives while educating the public and media on this cause.

K. knows his organization does not have the capacity to host such an important event. He then considers that joining forces with FC. (the organization of his new friends and colleagues F. and C.) could be a solution.

F. and C. are delighted by the idea and take on the partnership offer. They all agree on a calendar and start working right away. K. starts looking for a venue, figures out the logistical costs and looks for sponsors. F. and C. are in charge of inviting speakers and preparing the content of the event.

K. is happy. Everything is moving fast and F. and C. seem to be very efficient. Until... the day they meet to put everything together. K. realizes F. and C. have approached over 50 companies instead of focusing on famous personalities and well-known speakers. Now, he cannot approach any of them to offer a sponsorship package, since a speaker cannot (in his mind) also be sponsoring the event financially. He believes the media will then think the content is biased. F. and C. have secured 35 speakers, all from small to medium size companies.

 K. doesn't know how to fit that many people into a one-day event, nor how to attract big media without famous speakers. No media, no sponsors. No sponsors, no event!

Long story short, the partners have to postpone the event and apologize to the 35 potential speakers. K. explains his vision to F. and C. in much more detail, and makes sure they are all fully aligned before trying again!

Ask Yourself

People cannot read your mind. Make sure you fully discuss these five key questions:
        1: What?
        2: When?
        3: Where?
        4: For Who?
        5: How much?

Take action

In order to avoid this pitfall, we challenge you to:

> *Leave lots of time for questions, and always ask your partner to reiterate his or her understanding of the plan after your initial discussion. Use the five questions above to make sure you don't forget anything!*

Pitfall #4 - Lack of Direction or Leadership

For a team's work to move forward, it is necessary to have a clear vision. This vision must translate into a clear action plan.

When projects are at a small scale, or when they are first getting started, decisions can be shared easily and an organization may not need one person to lead. However, on a larger scale an initiative without clear leadership can be slowed down by a lack of direction.

Example

D. and G. have been best friends since kindergarten. Although they took different paths after high school, they are now excited to be working together on a fantastic project, fighting against homeless exclusion and misperception through photography.

D. and G. do everything together. From training homeless people to take photographs to pitching the project to top art galleries, they share the work 50/50.

Between both the good days and the bad days, they face them and celebrate them together. They even do the accounting together!

D. and G. both have strong personalities, so neither would do well with the other taking the lead. But so far, so good!

The project starts building momentum and gets noticed, and they receive their first request for an interview in the local press. They insist on being interviewed together despite the journalist requesting to quote only one representative. Nonetheless, when the interview comes out they feel so proud!

This interview is the starting point of a path they had not envisioned. Five galleries ask to move forward with the negotiation of their offer simultaneously, the Mayor invites them for a meeting, they receive letters of support, invitations to meet with regional and national associations, and more.

Their project is ready to scale, but D. and G. are not ready to split the work. Who gets to meet with the Mayor? Who gets to represent the initiative at the national conference on social innovation? Who gets the final decision on deals with the galleries?

If they continue to do everything together, they won't be able to take on all the opportunities that could help their initiative and impact grow.

"A boat doesn't go forward if each one is rowing their own way."

Swahili proverb

Ask Yourself

As you put the project's future before your ego:
> What do you want to have the lead on when the project gets bigger?
> What are you OK to 'only' have a consultative voice on?
> Would your partner be OK to take the lead on that?

Take Action

In order to avoid this pitfall, we challenge you to:

> *Take a pen and paper and decide: on a larger scale, who will get to be the face of the project? Who will have the final decisions on what?*

Pitfall #5 - Clashing Work Styles

One of the most difficult parts of working together is working together with *different* people.

We all attach different values, norms, and importance to the work we do. Yet, being able to work with people who are different from you is a key to move your impact forward: it will give you complimentary perspectives on each challenge you face and allow more open and creative problem resolution.

"Conflict is inevitable, but combat is optional."

Max Lucade

Example

S. has always been independent. He likes taking on new projects and feels most productive when in a calm environment with as few distractions as possible. He is very committed to his work in general, and even more now that he owns his own company, a social business supporting refugees to become entrepreneurs.

S. has been contacted by a large corporation willing to help him scale his impact as part of their CSR (Corporate Social Responsibility) strategy. Delighted, he accepts the collaboration and drafts a new impact forecast for the coming year.

Rapidly, he realizes working with this large corporation adds a lot of complexity to his impact creation. Not only does he now have to document all of his activity, but he finds himself having to attend endless meetings where decisions are almost never final. Everything has to be approved, verified, and accounted for. What he used to do in one day now takes up to two weeks!

In addition to bureaucracy, S. starts to resent his new colleagues. Compared with his very committed, high-intensity work style he now has to work with smart but employee-minded people who seem to care more about their lunch break and holidays than getting things done.

Six months later, S. is still collaborating with this large corporation but adapts his work hours dedicated to this aspect of his business to better match the work capacity of his partners.

Ask Yourself

> What is a 'normal' work intensity for you?
> How do you like to collaborate when working within a team (Independently? Co-dependently?)

Take Action
In order to avoid this pitfall, we challenge you to:

> Pay attention to *how* you want to work, as much as *with who* and *on what*. Share this ideal work style with your collaborators, while remaining flexible to accept their ideal working styles too!

Pitfall # 6 - Lack of Formalization

A collaboration is like a marriage. It all starts out with a crush, or a will to work together, then there are 'dates' where collaborators put their ideas into actions. And eventually, collaborators can formally commit to sticking together... for the good days, and the bad days too!

Just like marriages, collaborations can be formalized. One best practice is to outline the collaboration in a written document such as a Memorandum of Understanding. This way, both parties agree how they will work together, and on any other parameters or implications that may arise in the future.

One common pitfall is not formalizing a collaboration or thinking it will go smoothly from the start and forever. When a challenge comes up it is important to have a previously agreed-upon guideline, or legal documentation, that covers how to move forward.

Example

J. is a fair trade entrepreneur. She helps single moms in Romania by employing them to craft recycled jewelry. One day she meets F., who owns an online ethical retail store in the United Kingdom. F. want to diversify the products he sells in his online shop and offers to distribute J.'s jewelry.

It goes really well! There is so much demand J. doubles her production and hires five new women just to keep up. Plus, the UK market is an opportunity to increase her prices to grow her impact. She invests the extra profit into school tuition for her worker's kids.

Little by little, J. only concentrates on F.'s retail store. Everything is agreed: the retail price, the margin, the quantity delivered. Everything? Well, they haven't really formalized a proper collaboration, but well, F. and J. get along so well!

Until one day F. has a car accident. He has to stop working. Doctors say he needs to rest for at least six months. F. had been approached by a social impact fund recently and decides to take them up on their offer; he sells his ethical retail store to them.

The fund decides to turn the strategy upside-down and only focus on locally-produced goods that have a local impact. They decide not to renew J.'s usual order.

Practically overnight, J. loses her partner and 100% of her orders vanish. Without any formal agreement, she cannot ask for a 60 or 90 day notice to give her some time to find new partners. She stops production until further notice and most single moms she used to employ have to urgently find backup jobs.

Ask Yourself

> How mature is the collaboration? How much time has been dedicated to it?
> Is the level of formalization in line with the maturity of your collaboration?

Take Action

In order to avoid this pitfall, we challenge you to:

> *Lookup Memorandum of Understanding examples online, so you have a guideline when you are ready to draft yours!*

In short, whether you choose to collaborate with a co-founder from scratch, or partner with other entities along the way, collaborations are key to solidify your impact as a social entrepreneur. The hard part is to make sure you can "stick together" in the long term!

Coming together is a beginning, staying together is progress, and working together is success.

Henry Ford

Here is a summary of the most common pitfalls, along with the questions you should answer and actions you can take!

How to Avoid the 6 Most Common Collaboration Pitfalls

1 - Collaborating "Just Because"

Ask yourself

What skills do you lack, that your ideal collaborator should have to help drive your initiative forward?

Take Action

Work on your own value proposition before inviting or accepting collaborators into your project. The more solid YOU are, the more solid collaborations will be in contributing to your impact.

2 - Misalignment of Goals

Ask yourself

What is your overall vision? Where do you see your initiative in 5 years?

Take Action

Share your vision with your potential and existing partners. Make sure they are flexible about the path you may take to achieve a clear vision you all agree on.

3 - Miscommunication and Misunderstandings

Ask yourself

What?
When?
Where?
For Who?
How much?

Take Action

Leave lots of time for questions, and always ask your partner to reiterate his or her understanding of the plan after your initial discussion. Use the five questions above to make sure you don't forget anything!

#4 - Lack of Direction or Leadership

Ask yourself
What do you want to have the lead on when the project gets bigger?

What are you OK to 'only' have a consultative voice on? Would your partner be OK to take the lead on that?

Take Action
Take a pen and paper and decide: on a larger scale, who will get to be the face of the project? Who will have the final decisions, on what?

5 - Clashing Work Styles

Ask yourself
What is a 'normal' work intensity for you?
How do you like to collaborate when working within a team (Independently? co-dependently?)

Take Action
Pay attention to *how* you want to work, as much as *with who* and *on what*. Share this ideal work style with your collaborators, while remaining flexible to accept their ideal working styles too!

6 - Lack of Formalization

Ask yourself
How mature is the collaboration? How much time has been dedicated to it?

Is the level of formalization in line with the maturity of your collaboration?

Take Action
Lookup Memorandum of Understanding examples online, so you have a guideline when you are ready to draft yours!

CHAPTER 5

Top 10 Collaboration Best Practices

CHAPTER 5 - TOP 10 COLLABORATION BEST PRACTICES

Tailor-made for Social Innovators and Changemakers

Now that you know what potential pitfalls to watch out for, let's focus on the best practices! As an introduction to this chapter, we are giving the floor to Rodd Wagner and Dr. Gale Muller, who have compiled their five years of research on collaboration and partnerships into the very inspiring *Power of 2* bestseller[12]. This book is about personal relationships as well as professional ones, and you will see that it works well with the Social Entrepreneur's collaborative mindset too.

"If you want to have great partnerships, be a great partner.

Get beyond yourself.

Give up the notion that you are well-rounded, and stop expecting your colleagues to be universally proficient.

Incorporate someone else's motivations into your view of the accomplishment.

Loosen up.

Focus more on what you do for the partnership than what you get from it.

Demonstrate trust and see if they don't surprise you with their trustworthiness.

Be slower to anger and quicker to forgive.

And along the way, communicate continuously."

Rodd Wagner and Dr. Gale Muller

---

[12] *Rodd Wagner and Gale Muller PhD, Power of 2: How to Make the Most of Your Partnerships at Work and in Life*

Inspired? Now, here is our Top 10 Collaboration Best Practices, tailor-made for social innovators and changemakers.

#1 - Work on Your Contribution

Collaborations are most fruitful when both partners come from a position of strength. You want collaborators to help fill your gaps, but it is important to also look at your individual strengths and develop them too.

This way you bring a strong, unique contribution to any partnership or collaboration you are involved with.

For Example:
- Is your expertise more specific than that of others in some way?
- Is your network something that could be of benefit to future partners?
- Do you have a large community (in real life or in social media)?
- Do you have a well-known name in your industry, or in a particular field?
- Can you offer a fresh perspective thanks to your own unique experiences?

Now that you have identified the specific ways you bring a strong contribution to a collaborative team, work on it.

Develop it, grow it, mention it in on your website and when you are interviewed. Become known for it, so that it becomes a great draw for potential partners to seek you out for collaborations!

#2 - Don't Put All Your Eggs in One Basket

Be intentional about who you want to partner with and why.

Consider how much time you are ready to dedicate to each collaboration, and recognize what portion of your *total* work time will be focused on this relationship to gauge its overall importance.

Remember to think 'lean' (Chapter 2 - Collaboration Roadmap) and grow your collaborations slowly over time. You do not want to dedicate 100% of your time to a collaboration with someone you barely know!

Also, give your partnerships the space and flexibility to adapt over time. In a co-founder type of partnership (where you dedicate 100% of your time and energy to a common project) make sure that the rules are clear from the beginning.

- If one person wants to (or has to) stop, what happens to the other?
- What can you do today (legally, but also not to lose knowledge, contacts, etc) to ensure a smooth transition if needed in the future?

#3 - Stay Clear on Your Goals and Objectives

If everyone is moving forward together, then success takes care of itself.

Henry Ford

Collaborations should be primarily grounded in a shared vision and shared understanding of the goals and mission. You can always figure out the *how* along the way, as long as the *why* is clear and aligned for all partners involved.

This is also useful when you need to make a big decision together. Perhaps you are looking at taking on a new opportunity together, need to mitigate a potential risk coming your way, or there is a desire to make a big change in the work.

- Will this action bring your collaboration closer to its objectives?
- Will it bring each partner closer to his or her own goals?

This requires everyone to be crystal clear on goals first and foremost. You can use the GROW framework outlined in the Bonus Resources at the end of this book to help guide this discussion with your collaborative team.

#4 - Be Transparent

When choosing who to collaborate with, stay honest in recognizing when you truly value their work and contribution to the project. If this appreciation - where each party recognizes the other fills a crucial gap - is not at the core, then there will likely be a disconnect that could jeopardize the collaboration.

It is harder than it sounds because it means being transparent and open about your own gaps, so you can fully display the appreciation you have for your collaborator. But since you also bring your unique set of strengths to the table (that you are constantly working on as explained in #1 above), it will be OK!

Transparency is not just a value, it should translate in your actions:
- Tell your collaborators *why* you like working with them;
- When you have doubts, or feel uncomfortable, say it! Don't expect people to guess what you are feeling;
- If you are in a managerial position, make it easy and safe for your team to be transparent (about both positive and negative things!).

If people work together in an open way with porous boundaries - that is, if they listen to each other and really talk to each other - then they are bound to trade ideas that are mutual to each other and be influenced by each other. That mutual influence and open system of working creates collaboration.

Richard Thomas

#5 - Communicate Clearly, From the Beginning

By communication, we mean two things:

1. Share out loud (what you think, feel, want, hope, believe, etc) through discussion or writing and,
2. Listen carefully (to the other person's thoughts, feelings, wills, hopes, beliefs, etc).

Communication is a two-way street!

Put into action, this means you have to dedicate *time* for communication. Organize meetings regularly; if possible do so when everyone has an open agenda so that it is not always just a quick update, but a chance for everyone to express his or her own view.

- How often are you going to meet? Once a month? Once a week?
- What is the goal of the discussion, or the desired outcome at the end of the meeting?
- What should partners prepare in advance for the discussion to be efficient and worthwhile?

The earlier you put a system in place to communicate (share and listen) clearly, the better chance your collaboration will have to succeed!

#6 - Communicate Clearly, When Things Go Bad

This is more difficult, yet even more important. Do not wait for the 'last drop' to make the situation explode! Ups and down are part of any social enterprise journey, and they certainly happen in collaborations.

When things start to look bad, the first step is *to communicate.*

Does this challenging moment mean you will give up? Or should you be scared the other one will want to give up if you speak out? NO! Or at least, not if you communicate early on. Communication is part of the healing process, and it is also part of resolution when there is conflict.

Try not to get overwhelmed by your own fears (of failing? of being left out?), and take the first step to communicate (share and listen), even if it is painful at first!

> *"Open, frank communication is the lynchpin to teamwork. A fractured team is like a fractured bone; fixing it is always painful and sometimes you have to re-break it to heal it fully – and the re-break always hurts more because it is intentional."*
>
> **Patrick Lencioni**

#7 - Communicate Clearly, When Things Go Well

This may sound like romantic advice, but it is truly important. Tell your partner how much you love working with them!

Don't reserve communication only for conflict or for updating the to-do list. Collaboration is like any human relationship; it requires mutual appreciation. Your partner may not know how much you appreciate them until you say it out loud, or let them know in writing!

Imagine the extra motivation collaborators can have when they often say to each other:

- How lucky they feel to be working together
- How much they appreciate each other's contributions
- How proud they are of the work completed together
- How motivated they feel to go the extra mile thanks to each other

The world of social entrepreneurship and social innovation is full of problem solvers. We, changemakers, have a special eye for challenges, a special heart for empathy, and a special brain for finding innovative solutions. We are fixers. We thrive on taking action and resolving situations. And all that is good.

But as the saying goes, we also have defects in our qualities. As fixing-oriented people, we sometimes forget to appreciate what is going well. We forget to fuel our relationships and collaborations with gratitude because we are too focused on what to do or what to solve next.

Remember the base of our motivation comes from gratitude, and energy comes from feeling appreciated. If you do not dedicate some time to fuel that motivation and energy with gratitude and appreciation, your collaboration will not go as far as it could solving social and environmental challenges.

#8 - Be Committed

Individual commitment to a group effort—that is what makes a team work, a company work, a society work, a civilization work.

Vince Lombardi

For a collaboration to be fruitful, you will need to work hard, put in the effort, go out of your comfort zone, make compromises, re-do things to fit with other's expectations, take risks, turn down opportunities, and so much more.

Why go through all that trouble? Because the goal worth it! *Not* only because you feel accountable to your partner, or afraid of what he or she might think of you if you do not follow through. Stay committed to moving forward toward your common goal!

This also means to not put too much pressure on your collaborator; take your individual responsibilities and *do your part*. Just like you would not like to be micromanaged, make sure you leave space for your partners to express their commitment, in their own creative way!

Be as committed to the work as you would like your partners to be. At the same time, do not compare your dedication with theirs, as it is their responsibility. As long as every individual does their part, and has the freedom to do it in each their own way, the collaboration should thrive!

#9 - Think Win/Win/Win

Sincere and generous collaboration is the best way to fulfil the legitimate aspirations of each person and achieve great collective goals for the common good and the general interest.

King Felipe VI

Creating results that are greater together than the sum of the parts is the magic of collaborations. Everyone should win, and not just each partner, but also the cause and the society as a whole.

How do you make this happen? Be intentional when driving your collaborative work forward and ask yourself:
- What do you have to win?
- What does your collaborator have to win?
- What does the society have to win?
- What can you *do*, so that these three 'wins' grow even bigger and faster?

#10 - Build Collaborations with Genuine, Authentic Motives

The *outcomes* of collaboration are a combination of what you win, what your partners win, and what society wins.

The process, however, is *not* about winning. It is about giving.
- What do you have to give?
- How can you contribute?
- How much time and energy are you willing to dedicate to this collaboration?

We chose to display this tip at the very end of this chapter, and after talking about the big picture 'win/win/win' outcome, on purpose.

If there is one thing to remember out of this chapter, and maybe even out of this book, it is one word: authenticity.

Be authentic about what motivates you, and what your goals are. Be authentic about what you do not want to do, and what bothers you or makes you feel uncomfortable.

Be yourself. Be ready to give part of yourself, and generously share what you have to share.

Have genuine motives, not artificial ones. Be there for the long run. Take your time, and give space for the collaboration to grow into its full potential.

No matter what happens, always stay true to yourself, and make your authenticity the center of each of your decisions.

To summarize, here are the Top 10 Best Practices, tailor-made for social innovators and changemakers, to drive fruitful collaborations (and change the world!):

1 - Work on Your Contribution
2 - Don't Put All Your Eggs in One Basket
3 - Stay Clear on Your Goals and Objectives
4 - Be Transparent
5 - Communicate Clearly, From the Beginning
6 - Communicate Clearly, When Things Go Bad
7 - Communicate Clearly, When Things Go Well
8 - Be Committed
9 - Think Win/Win/Win
10 - Build Collaborations with Genuine, Authentic Motives

In closing of this chapter, here is an excellent quote by the American Philosopher, Journalist, and poet Henry David Thoreau:

"It takes two to speak the truth –
one to speak, and another to hear."

Henry David Thoreau

CHAPTER 6

Looking Towards Collaboration on a Larger Scale

CHAPTER 6 - LOOKING TOWARDS COLLABORATION ON A LARGER SCALE

We need to develop and disseminate an entirely new paradigm and practice of collaboration that supersedes the traditional silos that have divided governments, philanthropies, and private enterprises for decades and replace it with networks of partnerships working together to create a globally prosperous society.

Simon Mainwaring

So far we have covered a lot of everyday practicalities for individual social entrepreneurs and small to medium sized social enterprises to leverage collaboration and grow reach and impact.

Now, we will touch on the types of large-scale collaborative opportunities you may encounter in the social innovation space. These collaboration strategies might not be in your near future, but it could be something you want to work towards, depending on the work you're doing to make a difference in the world.

The two main large-scale, formally structured collaborations are: Joint Ventures, and Collective Impact Initiatives.

Both of these strategies connect partners across public, private and even government sectors, where partners are very aligned towards a specific and often audacious goal. One that can only be accomplished thanks to the purposeful partnership of many key players who strategically coordinate their efforts to accomplish something HUGE!

Collective Impact Initiatives are a unique type of collaboration where many organizations (in some cases hundreds) come together to align themselves with shared goals and objectives within a complex social challenge, such as education or community health.

This type of collaboration is complex and requires a long-term time commitment from everyone involved. It also requires a dedicated 'backbone' organization or steering committee to guide the process in order for it to be successful. Given the need for a central organization or committee and the long timeline of collaboration, it can be challenging to find financial support for a collective impact initiative to take form. But funders are realizing the unique role they can play to support collective impact financially and strategically.[13]

Recent success in collective impact initiatives, such as Strive's work transforming education in the United States, provides great learning and hope for this type of collaboration to continue succeeding in the future in the world of social change. Joint Ventures, such as the one between Muhammad Yunus' Grameen Bank and the Danone food company, are long-term partnerships, often between a large (global) corporation and a social mission organization.

Joint Ventures

"Diverse groups of problem solvers outperformed the groups of the best individuals at solving complex problems. The reason: the diverse groups got stuck less often than the smart individuals, who tended to think similarly."

~ Scott E. Page

---

[13] *Lori Bartczak, "The Role of Grantmakers in Collective Impact", Stanford Social Innovation Review,*
http://ssir.org/articles/entry/the_role_of_grantmakers_in_collective_im pact

A Joint Venture is a long-term collaboration where two or more organizational partners come together and agree to jointly form a brand new legal company that is (usually) equally owned by the partners.

As you can imagine, it is a huge commitment to form a new company - one that requires it's own governance, executive team, staff, financing, operational procedures and so on.

Because a joint venture is formed by two pre-existing organizations, who often play an integral role as suppliers or partners to the new Joint Venture, the new company begins in a stronger position than a 'fresh start-up' would, but the scenario still poses some risks.

A Strategic Alliance can be similar to a joint venture but is a long-term relationship where no new corporate entity is created to carry out the work.

One well-known example of a successful Joint Venture in the social impact space is Grameen Danone. Let's look at how they got started and the impact these two organizations have had on malnutrition by working together.

Grameen Danone Foods Ltd.

In an interview with Franck Riboud, Chairman and CEO of Danone Group, he explains how a meeting with Muhammad Yunus ended in a handshake that would be the beginning of the Grameen Danone Foods Ltd. Joint Venture.[14]

Since it was founded in 2006, the mission of Grameen Danone Foods Ltd has been to "reduce poverty by bringing health through food to children using a unique community-based business model."[15]

---

[14] *"An interview on social business with Franck Riboud, Chairman and CEO, Danone Group", https://www.youtube.com/watch?v=hC5Wz3_tnnA*
[15] *"Grameen Danone Foods Ltd - Nutrition",*
http://www.yunussb.com/grameen-danone-foods-ltd-nutrition/

Yunus, with his social business model to fight poverty, and Riboud, with his expertise in food products, joined forces to produce a new type of yogurt - one that has critical nutrients and is also affordable, even to the poorest of the poor. In addition to developing a product that delivers needed nutrition at a reasonable price point, the joint venture is a true social business where with every decision, social and environmental impact are top of mind.

The business model is designed so that:

- milk used in the yogurt is purchased from micro-farmers.
- the yogurt is distributed through a door-to-door sales model where sales ladies earn 10% of sales.
- unsold yogurts are bought back.
- the production plant is partially powered by solar energy.
- the yogurt packaging is fully biodegradable.

Not only has the Joint Venture has been key in the creation of roughly 1,600 jobs near it's original plant (with plans to expand significantly) but the impact of the product is positive. An independent NGO's testing found that children consuming their nutrient-rich yogurt once a day over a year resulted in improved IQ and growth indicators.[16]

"The best opportunities to partner are those very core to your business: distribution, service development, and the like."

Nat Robinson, Juhudi Kilimo

---

[16] *"Grameen Danone Foods Ltd - Nutrition"*

Collective Impact

"Not being a genius, I believe in collaboration, and my background as a problem solver means I've never been afraid to work with people cleverer than myself."

Daniel Barber

Collective Impact is a powerful collaboration strategy that was first introduced by John Kania and Mark Kramer in a 2011 article in the Stanford Social Innovation Review.[17]

The idea of collective impact is to align several (sometimes hundreds) individuals and organizations of all sizes and across sectors, around a single cause. The approach was developed when leaders realized that no one organization, no matter how good at their job they were, would be able to dramatically improve outcomes on their own.

Social issues, like education, require massive coordination across the spectrum of people who serve young people in a geographic area to really make a difference.

As Kania and Kramer describe, the collective impact initiative, Strive, had the "ambitious mission… to coordinate improvements at *every* stage of a young person's life, from "cradle to career"".

As outlined in the Stanford Social Innovation Review's 2012 article on the subject, the five key conditions for achieving large-scale change with Collective impact are:

> **Common Agenda:** All participants have a shared vision for change including a common understanding of the problem and a joint approach to solving it through agreed upon actions.

---

[17] *Kania and Kramer, "Collective Impact"*

Shared Measurement: Collecting data and measuring results consistently across all participants ensures efforts remain aligned and participants hold each other accountable.

Mutually Reinforcing Activities: Participant activities must be differentiation while still being coordinated through a mutually reinforcing plan of action.

Continuous Communication: Consistent and open communication is needed across the main players to build trust, assure mutual objectives, and appreciate common motivation.

Backbone Support: Creating and managing collective impact requires a separate organization(s) with staff and a specific set of skills to serve as the backbone for the entire initiative and coordinate participating organizations and agencies.

From the Stanford Social Innovation Review [18]

There is a lot to learn and understand about collective impact, but for the purposes of this book, we are going to keep it personal and look at a case study where a collective impact approach is making a difference for early childhood development in Calgary, Alberta, Canada.

Collective Impact Case Study: First 2000 Days

First 2000 Days is a network that uses a collective impact strategy to improve early childhood development.[19]

Their mission is: to enable unique contributions from a diverse group of individuals and organizations to achieve the vision of the First 2000 Days Network by acting as a catalyst for learning, connecting, and collaborative action.

---

[18] *Shiloh Turner, Kathy Merchant, John Kania and Ellen Martin, "Understanding the Value of Backbone Organizations in Collective Impact: Part 1, Stanford Social Innovation Review, July 17, 2012,* http://ssir.org/articles/entry/understanding_the_value_of_backbone_or ganizations_in_collective_impact_1
[19] *First 2000 Days Network, http://www.2000days.ca*

The first 2000 days of a child's life is a crucial time for brain development. Supporting development throughout this time has shown that children experience better outcomes in areas related to school, health, relationships, society and communication.

For this reason, focusing early childhood development efforts through collective impact is a powerful strategy to bring lasting impact for these youth.[20]

The First 2000 Days Network website houses a wealth of information where you can learn more about what they do, as well as access further collective impact resources.[21]

Interview with Alix Linaker

We had the pleasure of sitting down with Alix Linaker, one of the members of the backbone structure for this collective impact initiative, to get her on-the-ground insight on what it's like to be a part of a cross-sectorial, system-wide collaboration.

Much of her insight is also taken from her experience with two other Calgary-based collective impact initiatives, The Dementia Network and the LD and ADHD Network.

Key learnings from our chat with Alix Linaker, Project Coordinator with Creating Value Inc. *(February 19, 2016)*

On the 5 Factors

"There's no one factor that's more important than the other. There might be times in the evolution of the initiative that one may be more important at a certain point in time. For example, shared measurement systems are so important, but at the very beginning, setting a common agenda is going to be more important. "

---

[20] *"Who We Are", First 2000 Days Network, http://www.2000days.ca/who-we-are*

[21] *"What We Do", First 2000 Days Network, http://www.2000days.ca/what-we-do*

"Because you can't have a shared measurement system until you have a common agenda…. Continuous communication is so important at all stages."

"You need to have everyone know what's going on, internally, and also having the messages going out to the public be consistent."

On Having a Common Agenda

"A common agenda keeps everyone in line, and it implies yes, we are all from different organizations, or different sectors, and some of these people may not traditionally talk or they may "compete", but they are coming together around the common agenda."

"You can bring insights from your own sectors or organizations, but at the end of the day, it's about the common agenda and working towards achieving the strategic goal."

On the Backbone Role

"The structural entity of the backbone can vary. For example, it could be one organization (as in the case of The Dementia Network), two organizations (as in the case of the LD and ADHD Network), or a collection of people from different organizations or initiatives that have come together to form the backbone (as in the case of the First 2000 Days Network). It can depend on the organization's capacities, people's capacities, and how much funding is received. There's no one way to set up an initiative. There's a lot of tailoring to what best suits needs, resources, and capacity."

"It is vital to have a clear vision and strategy from the beginning. In collective impact literature, the first key role of the backbone is to guide vision and strategy. It's important to have people dedicated to guiding this and ensuring all members of the initiative are on the same page. Yes, people are from different organizations and sectors, but they're there advancing the common agenda that's been set for the initiative. The priority is the common agenda for the initiative."

On Structure

"Traditionally there's a Steering Committee to guide the strategic direction of the initiative, and any changes are typically approved by a consensus."

"Out of that Steering Committee there can be Action Teams or Working Groups."

"They can include people from the Steering Committee, but also others who are interested and have expertise in a certain Action Team's focus area, for example, public awareness or advocacy."

On Process

"It sounds simple, but having one person dedicated to setting up and maintaining project management platforms such as Google Drive, Basecamp, or Dropbox (or whatever the platform is), is important."

"In my experience, it's difficult to get everyone to consistently use the structures processes, such as online project management platforms, that are put in place. Why that's critical is because it's easy to miss information if not everyone is using the same communication system. Something as simple as making sure everyone is receiving the calendar invites is important for ensuring continuous communication."

On Communication

"Constant, continuous open communication is crucial. The backbone is a key supporter of that communication. It also involves setting up structures and processes that keep everything organized and remind people why they're there and the direction the initiative is going. For example, The Dementia Network sends out monthly internal updates to ensure everyone is aware of what is happening in the initiative as a whole."

"The First 2000 Days Network sends an external facing newsletter to their community of followers. You also need to make sure everyone's receiving the right information at the right time because it comes back to the common agenda and the shared vision and strategy; you need to ensure everyone is on the same wavelength to ensure the initiative is moving at the right pace and in the right direction."

On Adaptability

"The First 2000 Days network doesn't have Action Teams anymore, and instead have Change Collectives. They've adapted the structure to fit their needs"

"The reason is that within the ECD sector, there's so much that exists already for it; they don't feel like they need to go in and actively create new resources. For example, there are geographic coalitions that do great ECD work. However, the ECD system needs to be better connected and supported, so everyone's talking, important connections are sparked, and partnerships are being made. But more than that, it's about systems-level change; shifting mindsets and practice that will impact the sector at the systemic level."

"The Network has evolved from the beginning and it's an example of why the ability to adapt is paramount. Adaptability is also important because the environment is constantly changing. For example, a change in government could have a significant impact on different social issues or funding available."

On Measuring Success

"In general terms, there's different success factors based on how far along the initiative is. First the backbone has to be guiding the vision and strategy and supporting the aligned activities. Then once that's set in motion, you can start establishing shared measurement practices, which is critical for the initiative to continue. Say you're doing this work and you're not really achieving anything or making a difference. Then people ask, "why are we doing this?". The shared measurement practices are important for having everyone on the same page about what's being measured and how it's being measured."

"In terms of backbone capacity, internally there may be people who are good at evaluation and shared measurement practices, or you might have to bring a consultant in. So it can be internal or external, but eventually everyone needs to understand the system and help use it."

What is your favorite thing about Collective Impact?

"I like that it brings together different sectors and people that would normally not work together, or that compete with each other around a common social issue. For example, there could be two nonprofits that are competing for funding and working in silos on the same issue, but their capacity would be so much greater if they worked together."

101

"That concept of, rather than competing, collaborating.Building capacity is such a key component of it, and capacity is a significant issue in the social sector because of limited money, funding, and revenue generation."

What is your advice to anyone jumping into a Collective Impact scenario?

"It's key to have patience. For example, many people are very action-oriented and want to jump into action right away.But you need time to ensure everything below the surface is set; time to create the strategy and common agenda, and to make those important connections. In other words, to set up the foundation, which is time-consuming in a complex initiative such as collective impact."

"It's essential to have action-oriented people, but it's also essential to have those people who can take a step back and make sure we have the foundation first. And since these are complex social issues that require systems-level change, the desired impact is going to take time. Because it's so complicated, it's key that from the beginning everyone has an understanding of what a system is, especially in context to the initiative they're a part of, and that they understand the issue in its wider context."

*"Teamwork is the ability to work together toward a common vision. The ability to direct individual accomplishments toward organizational objectives.
It is the fuel that allows common people to attain uncommon results." Andrew Carnegie*

Further Readings

Acumen, a global non-profit organization working to change the world tackles poverty through impact investing, speaks about partnering with global organizations.

In their report, Collaborating for Growth with Impact, they identify three partnership models where relatively small social enterprises can collaborate with global companies.

1 - Skills Partnership
2 - Channel Partnership
3 - Venture Partnership

Take a look at the report to learn more about this and for further background on how relatively small social enterprises can partner with global corporations to grow their impact. [22]

For more information on Collective Impact, you can browse these in-depth articles:

- Channeling Change: Making Collective Impact Work :
http://ssir.org/articles/entry/channeling_change_making_collective_impact_work

- Aligning Collective Impact Initiatives :
http://ssir.org/articles/entry/aligning_collective_impact_initiatives

- Essential Mindset Shifts for Collective Impact :
http://ssir.org/articles/entry/essential_mindset_shifts_for_collective_impact

- Defining Quality Collective Impact :
http://ssir.org/articles/entry/defining_quality_collective_impact

---

[22] *"Social Enterprises and Global Corporations Collaborating for Growth with Impact", Acumen, 2015, http://acumen.org/wp-content/uploads/2015/10/1502_AcumenSummitReport_092115Finalv2_pgs.pdf*

- The Value of Backbone Organizations in Collective Impact : http://ssir.org/articles/entry/understanding_the_value_of_backb one_organizations_in_collective_impact_1

- Power Dynamics in Collective Impact : http://ssir.org/articles/entry/power_dynamics_in_collective_imp act

- Embracing Emergence: How Collective Impact Addresses Complexity : (http://ssir.org/articles/entry/embracing_emergence_how_collec tive_impact_addresses_complexity)

It is the long history of humankind (and animal kind, too) those who learned to collaborate and improvise most effectively have prevailed.

Charles Darwin

CONCLUSION

As you navigate through the rest of your life, be open to collaboration. Other people and other people's ideas are often better than your own. Find a group of people who challenge and inspire you, spend a lot of time with them, and it will change your life.

Amy Poehler

As a social entrepreneur with a 'heart for the world' it can be tempting to stretch yourself to every corner, innovating new solutions at every turn to the challenges you see around you.

However, you will find that when you set your focus squarely on the vision for change you wish to see in the world, harnessing your precious smarts, time and resources towards that end, over time you will truly see a shift for the better.

Because don't forget - alongside you are many thousands of changemakers all working towards *their* visions for change, and giving their unique skills and talents back to the world.

Collaboration and partnerships allow you to keep your focus while at the same time leveraging the focus of others when and how you need it to advance your mission. This symbiotic give and take results in big wins for you, your collaborators, *and* society as a whole.

Hopefully clearer now than ever before you realize how powerful a tool collaboration is for the social entrepreneur's journey in achieving lasting change.

We hope you found value in this collection of practical advice to help you grow your impact to new heights thanks to this 'secret superpower'.

Now that you are armed with greater understanding of types of collaborations, a step-by-step collaboration roadmap, the most common pitfalls and best practices, and numerous examples - go out to find your dream partners and make an impact!

The wonderful work of a social entrepreneur is never over! So enjoy the ride and remember...

"If you want to go fast, go alone.
If you want to go far, go with others."

African proverb

All the best,

Danielle & Solène

PS - We would love to hear your collaboration stories and learning! Share your insights in the <u>Global Social Entrepreneurs Lab group on Facebook</u>, or find us at <u>www.globalsocentlab.com</u>.

Bonus Resources!

QUESTIONS TO ASK / ANSWER WHEN EXPLORING A NEW POTENTIAL PARTNERSHIP

USING THE GROW FRAMEWORK FOR COLLABORATION

EMAIL INTRODUCTION SCRIPT

★

TOOLS FOR COLLABORATION

QUESTIONS
TO ASK / ANSWER

When Exploring a New Potential Partnership

Here are guidelines to help you make the most of your initial collaboration meetings! The questions we selected might sound like questions you would get asked at a job interview... But at the end of the day, isn't a job interview a collaboration between an individual and an organization?

Just like HR people do, look beyond the answers: do you trust the person in front of you? Do you feel in your gut that you would like to work with he or she?

Last advice - if you have doubts, worries, or reservations, say them out loud! Give your potential partners the chance to address those issues (or not!).

FOR COLLABORATION WITH AN INDIVIDUAL:

Vision for the partnership
- Why are you interested in this partnership?
- What do you think this partnership can bring to you?
- What do you think you can bring to this partnership?

Understanding the profile & values
- What did you study (at university), and why?
- What do you do today, and what do you like about it?
- Why is this cause (social impact created/willing to be created) important to you personally?

Action Style
- Who else are/did you collaborating with?
- What collaboration example are you especially proud of?
- Who do you LOVE working with? Why?
- What is your biggest failure?
- In 5 years, what do you want this collaboration to look like?

FOR COLLABORATION WITH ANOTHER ORGANIZATION:

Vision for the partnership
- Why are you interested in this partnership?
- What do you think this partnership can bring to you?
- What do you think you can bring to this partnership?

Understanding the profile and values
- What is the story of the organization? When and why was it started?
- What is the mission of the organization today?
- How do you see this collaboration fit into the overall mission of your org?

Action style
- Who else have you collaborated with?
- What collaboration example are you especially proud of?
- What is your organization's biggest failure?
- In 5 years, what do you want this collaboration to look like?

PS: Don't be scared to lead the discussion, even if you are a small organization discussing with a big organization. You have more to lose if things go south, so don't be scared to be demanding. Plus, it will make you look very involved and reliable!

USING THE
GROW FRAMEWORK
FOR COLLABORATION

This simple framework can be helpful for collaborators to go through the goal setting process, and get 'on the same page' in terms of arriving at a shared agenda. It is a popular model used by coaches and leaders to set strong goals, problem-solve, and think through decisions.

There are a few versions of the framework, but in essence GROW is an acronym for:

GOAL

REALITY

OPTIONS (+ OBSTACLES)

WAY FORWARD

In the beginning stages of your collaboration, sit down as a group and use the following questions to guide your discussion. By the end you should have uncovered any concerns, and arrive at a clear path for moving the project forward.

GOAL - What is the SMART goal that the collaborators are working towards?

Remember to articulate specific outcomes (specific), how you will know when you reach it (measurable), a scope that is not too broad (achievable), a goal that is in alignment for all partners (relevant), and to articulate the timelines (time-bound).

REALITY - What is the current reality faced?

Discuss the current situation, including each partner's motivations for coming together, and the strengths, opportunities and constraints each is bringing to the table.

OPTIONS - What are the possible paths you can take forward?

Now that the team is clear on their common goal, and have examined the current reality, at this point you want to brainstorm all of the various possibilities and paths for how you could move forward towards achieving the goal.

The 'O' in GROW is also interpreted as **Obstacles.** So you can take some time at this stage to ask the group what potential obstacles they foresee and use this as an opportunity to take those into account as you determine your action steps in the next step.

WAY FORWARD - What action steps is each partner willing to commit to?

This step is important! Now that you have gathered so much useful information in your discussion, you need to translate it into the specific actions each person will take. These actions should of course lead the team back to the SMART goal within the agreed upon timeframe.

Resources for using the GROW Model:

- https://en.wikipedia.org/wiki/GROW_model
- https://www.mindtools.com/pages/article/newLDR_89.htm

EMAIL
INTRODUCTION SCRIPT

After some time getting to know each other, you may feel ready to reach and ask someone to take on a small project together.

Your first time reaching out should have the following:

> Show that it's a personal request by mentioning something specific relating to the person you're contacting,
> Set the stage with some background on your current situation so the person understands the context of your proposal,
> Propose your idea,
> Touch on how it could be a win/win opportunity for all involved (answer the "what's in it for them" question!),
> Let them know you're open to discuss the idea so it can be a great fit for both of you,
> Leave an 'out' so that they won't feel obligated to say yes if it's not the right time, or not a good fit for whatever reason.

Just for fun, here's a look back in time to the email that kicked off the Creators for Good / the Sedge collaborative journey:

Hi Solène,

Hope you have been well! How is your Turkish coming?

I had a flash of an idea the other day and wanted to reach out to you to see if you might be interested.

I was thinking that I would love to host a live Q&A event for Social Entrepreneurs (online). It could be webinar style, audio teleseminar, or even a simple live twitter chat (something I haven't tried before but sounds like fun). I'm thinking of having a few prepared questions to kick things off and then take questions from the audience for the rest of the period.

Then I thought of you! Would you like to join me? Creators for Good and theSedge.org (you and I) can co-host! I think it makes the dynamic a bit more fun for attendees because they get to hear two perspectives so it's like a "mini" speakers panel. Plus we can invite both our communities to join in and essentially double up our marketing reach. It will be great list building for each of us as well.

The reason I feel this could be a good win-win opportunity is that occurred to me that our offerings are quite complementary. You offer one-on-one strategic coaching programs and my BOOST Academy is self-guided with less one-on-one coaching (hardly any, just 30 minutes as a bonus). BOOST is a lesser investment but doesn't necessarily deliver on the personalized solutions or accountability. It's more for the 'do it yourself-er' who wants to understand how their social enterprise idea could take shape, but may not even be ready to dive into full implementation (or is ready to implement but has more experience taking action with an idea so needs less coaching).

Anyways, let me know what you think. I am completely open to any changes to this idea and if it doesn't feel like the right fit for you at this time, no worries! I completely understand if it doesn't fit into your overall strategy so no hard feelings either way :)

Take care and talk to you soon!

Danielle

There you go! It could have been a bit shorter, but since we had met for a "Skype coffee" already, there was already some trust and rapport built.

Feel free to adapt this outline when you approach a potential collaborator with a proposal. Remember, if you're feeling shy and not quite sure what to say, just be yourself. You really can't go wrong if you are open, friendly, and considerate. Good luck!

TOOLS
FOR COLLABORATION

With today's technology, collaborative projects can be more seamlessly managed than ever before.

Especially with larger teams, taking the time to set up *and use* a process for communicating and managing workflow can have a huge impact on the success of the collaboration.

Here's a list of our favorite (mostly free) tools to help manage your collaborations. If there's a tool you love using that's not on the list, be sure to post it in the Global Social Entrepreneurs Lab!

For General Planning:

★ Google calendar - Book meetings and key dates on a shared calendar no one misses a beat.

For Task Management:

★ Trello - Our top choice for organizing tasks, ideas, and lists for shared projects. It's free too!

★ Asana & Basecamp - More robust task management systems that have tons of features. Both free and paid options available.

For Content Management:

★ Google Drive - Save your documents in the cloud and allow everyone to edit (even at the same time) or comment. This will literally save you hours of time and confusion not having to send multiple versions back and forth by email. There is also a built-in version history in case past work needs to be recovered. But the best thing? Thanks to auto-saving, no work is ever lost when your computer crashes!

★ Evernote - Clip anything and everything from the Internet into notes that can be saved and organized for later reference.

★ Dropbox - It's like a virtual hard drive where you can upload and download files that need to be easily accessed by anyone on the project at anytime. Again, no need send countless emails with more attachments than you can count (or fit within email file size limits).

For Communication:

★ Skype - Free audio and video conferencing. Our go-to choice for "Skype coffees" with friends and colleagues around the world.

★ Appear.in - Another videoconference option where you can invite up to 8 people into a 'room' with you.

★ Slack - A tool where you can organize group chats by themes and topics.

Note : If you have other favorite tools for collaboration, share it with us and other Social Entrepreneurs in our facebook group : Global Social Entrepreneurs Lab
https://www.facebook.com/groups/1698669003694897/

THANK YOU

We want to express our gratitude once again to Alix Linaker, Project Coordinator with Creating Value Inc. for sharing her insights and experience, for our chapter on "Looking Towards Collaboration on a Larger Scale" !

And BIG thanks to our kind community members who helped with proofreading this collaborative book!

Andrea Wall

Benjamin Masila

Bill Fillner

Camille Bossel

Cristina Basto

Faiza Hajji Wozniak

Julia Marczi

Juliet Le Breton

Karen Johnson

Lujain Said Baghouth

Margaret O'Brien De Murillo

Matthew Johnsen

Mike Britton

Natalie Crüe

Rita Golstein-Galperin

Sara Soph Ost

Tara Anderson

Thomas Fontaine

Umesh Kumar

Danielle & Solène

www.ingramcontent.com/pod-product-compliance
Lightning Source LLC
Chambersburg PA
CBHW060347190526
45169CB00002B/515